IMAGES
of America

ITALIANS OF PHILADELPHIA

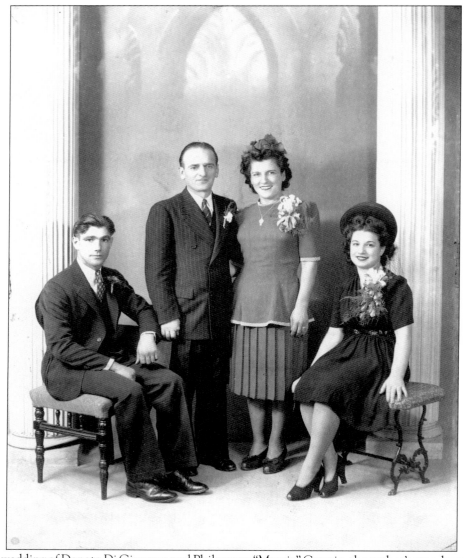

The wedding of Donato Di Giacomo and Philomena "Mamie" Cesario, the author's grandparents, took place on September 26, 1942. Born and raised in the Italian settlement of Germantown, they represented the two main groups of Italians who settled in the neighborhood: his family was from the province of Salerno in the region of Campania, and her family was from the province of Cosenza in the region of Calabria. They resided in the Italian area of Twenty-second and Clearfield Streets. The best man is Charles Manuola, of North Philadelphia, and maid of honor is Mary Cibotti, originally of South Philadelphia.

On the cover: From left to right, John Casella, Salvatore Mignogna, Tony Micale, and, in rear, Mike Albanese play bocce at Tenth and Fitzwater Streets in South Philadelphia. Similar to croquet, the person with the ball nearest to the target jack wins. Played since ancient Roman times, and primarily by men, it was one of many ways immigrants were able to enjoy Old World comforts while adjusting to a new country. (Courtesy of Temple University Libraries, Urban Archives.)

IMAGES
of America

ITALIANS OF
PHILADELPHIA

Donna J. Di Giacomo

ARCADIA
PUBLISHING

Published by Arcadia Publishing
Charleston SC, Chicago IL, Portsmouth NH, San Francisco CA

Printed in the United States of America

Library of Congress Catalog Card Number: 2007921754

For all general information contact Arcadia Publishing at:
Telephone 843-853-2070
Fax 843-853-0044
E-mail sales@arcadiapublishing.com
For customer service and orders:
Toll-Free 1-888-313-2665

Visit us on the Internet at www.arcadiapublishing.com

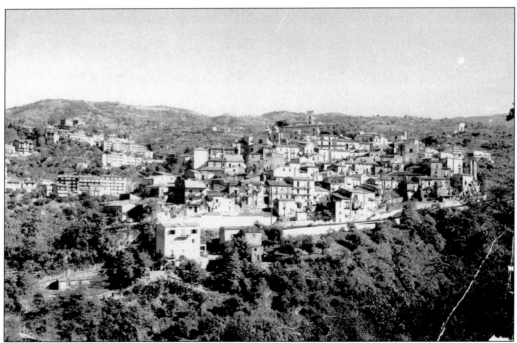

Here is a panorama view of Luzzi, Cosenza, Calabria, Italy. Most of the immigrants from this town settled in Germantown, with later immigrants settling in East Falls and Chestnut Hill, all in the northwest section of the city. Italian immigrants came from small towns such as Luzzi, settling in large cities because of jobs and the promise of future economic improvement.

CONTENTS

ACKNOWLEDGMENTS

It has been said many times, but it bears repeating: writing a book is truly a group effort. One person just cannot do it alone.

In the course of putting together this volume, I have met many wonderful people, and I hope it is the start of many lifelong friendships and collaborations.

There are so many people to thank: my editor, Erin Vosgien, who is just fantastic and was a pleasure to work with; my parents, Donald and MaryAnn, for their encouragement and enthusiasm; my brother, Donny, for just being him; and my dear cousin Norman, who was my rock throughout this project (as he is every day). He gave me many tips to overcome the anxiety. Saying "thank you" is really not enough.

I also met many people who were eager to help with this project. These people are very knowledgeable and enthusiastic about their neighborhoods. They are, in no particular order, Louis Iatorola of the Historical Society of Tacony, who so graciously offered me the society's Italian archives (it was through him that Tacony's Italians are well represented here); pastor Fr. John Large and parishioners of Mater Dolorosa Parish, all of whom contributed timeless images as poignant reminders of the Italians of Frankford; Denise Di Antonio, whose beautiful vintage pictures will give readers a glimpse into the Italians of Twenty-second and Clearfield Streets in North Philadelphia; and also John and everyone else at Temple University's Urban Archives, whose helpfulness and knowledge made each visit a pleasant and memorable experience. I would also like to thank Lou Arata, Joanne Strollo, Chenza Iannuzzi Cerrato, and everyone else who contributed photographs. Thanks also to Dr. Vincenza Scarpaci of the University of Oregon, who gave me great suggestions.

Finally, I owe an immense debt to historian and scholar Celeste A. Morello, M.A., M.S. She gave me unique suggestions regarding overlooked and underappreciated South Philadelphia landmarks. I cannot say enough about her vigorous and tireless efforts to keep history alive and well. To say I am eternally indebted to her would be quite the understatement.

And I could never forget to thank the editorial department of the *Philadelphia Daily News* for keeping my name in its op-ed pages for the past 16 years.

This book is dedicated to all Italian immigrants who bravely left the land of their ancestors to face a radically different life and who overcame numerous obstacles to become successful—in both big and small ways.

The Pennsylvania historical markers featured in this book are a registered trademark of the Pennsylvania Historical and Museum Commission, and the marker text is copyrighted material.

The following titles are suggested for further reading:

Biagi, Ernest L. *The Italians of Philadelphia.* New York: Carlton Press, 1967.
Di Stasi, Lawrence, ed. *Una Storia Segreta: The Secret History of Italian American Evacuation and Internment During World War II.* Berkley, CA: Heyday Books, 2001.
Grito, Richard D., and Anthony F. Noto. *Italian Presence in Pennsylvania.* University Park, PA: Pennsylvania Historical Association, 1990.
Weigley, Russell F. ed. Philadelphia, A 300-Year History. New York: W. W. Norton and Company, 1982.

INTRODUCTION

The story of Italian immigration to the United States is complex. It is one that will never be fully told.

The reason for the mass exodus of Italians looks simple on paper—economic stress after the so-called unification of Italy in 1861—but, in reality, the story is much more complex, mainly due to vast regional differences.

Italy has only been a unified country twice in its history: first during the Roman Empire and in recent times, since the 1861 unification. In the period after the fall of Rome until the 1861 unification under the House of Savoia (Savoy), a patchwork of kingdoms, duchies, republics, city-states, and principalities coexisted alongside the so-called Holy Roman Empire.

This political fragmentation led to the profound regional differences that exist to this day within present-day Italy—culturally, linguistically, gastronomically, economically, and in every other way. And the regional differences run deep to this day with many influences: in the north, there exists German, French, and Slavic influences, and in the south, Greek, Spanish, Albanian, and Arabic influences remain, hundreds and thousands of years later.

Italians of Philadelphia focuses on the immigrants who hailed primarily from small towns and villages of the regions of the south, known as the *meridione* and the *mezzogiorno*, corresponding to the late Kingdom of the Two Sicilies, ruled by the Spanish Bourbons until 1861. This book focuses on the lives of the everyday immigrants and their families as they attempted to establish themselves in a new country and society, while attempting to maintain some sort of connection with the towns, villages, and provinces they left behind.

The churches, stores, social clubs, and festivals that, in many cases, continue to exist to this day are proof of this continuity and, at the same time, are evidence of a creation that is no longer solely Italian in the true sense of the word but fits more in that category called Italian American, for lack of a better term.

In some instances, regional dialects, while disappearing in Italy itself, have survived in many Italian American households in Philadelphia and Little Italies throughout the United States, even if influenced by the English language. This is a further example of the unique by-product of the Italian immigrant experience.

Philadelphia's Italian neighborhoods reflect many of these aspects of the immigrant experience. Most especially, immigrants from particular provinces of Italy tended to settle in certain neighborhoods and surround themselves with churches and clubs primarily populated by their beloved *paesani*, who hailed from the same town or province in Italy. Although certain town names are mentioned in connection with certain neighborhoods, it is important to remember that immigrants from nearly every province of southern Italy also settled in that area.

Time and again, southern Italian immigrants are collectively referred to as peasants, farmers, and/or illiterate. Numerous volumes make it seem as if southern Italians just crawled out from under a rock and decided to board a boat and make a go of it in another country.

It is important to establish that southern Italians came to the United States not due to religious or political persecution but because of the promise of more money. They were looking to improve their economic standing in life. Many achieved their goal and went back to Italy to stay while many more decided to stay put in the United States. The poorest of the poor could not afford to make one trip on a boat let alone keep paying for return trips back and forth between Italy and the United States (which is what many immigrants did). They came to the United States trained as stonemasons, blacksmiths, shoemakers, cabinetmakers, and so on. The main problem was that the infrastructure of the United States was already built up (unlike that of Brazil and Argentina) by the time the waves of mass immigration began hitting American shores, so there was no need for those skills, for the most part (whereas Brazil and Argentina benefited from skilled Italian labor in order to build up their countries).

And although these people may not have been that of letters, they could hardly be classified as illiterate or ignorant. The vast majority of those southern Italian immigrants took almost immediately to another language, one that was radically different from their native tongue in every sense of the word, and even though they may have retained an accent, they became fluent in it. There were many immigrants throughout the city who spoke multiple languages fluently while their critics, and, sadly, some of their descendents, are far from bilingual.

At one time, Philadelphia was able to support more than a few Italian-language radio broadcasts and was home to a few Italian-language newspapers, including *L'Opinione*, *Il Popolo Italiano*, *La Libera Parola*, *Ordine Nuovo* (the Sons of Italy newspaper), the *Italian-American Herald*, and even *Vita*—the Italian-language newspaper of the United Presbyterian Church.

Italians have been populating Philadelphia, albeit in much smaller numbers than what the waves of mass immigration would send, since Colonial times. In his 1998 book *Building Little Italy, Philadelphia's Italians Before Mass Migration*, Villanova University professor of sociology Richard N. Juliani thoroughly documented the Colonial and early-Victorian Italian community of South Philadelphia, the first person to do so. There is a plethora of books that have been written over time regarding South Philadelphia's various Italian settlements, and there remain many Italian landmarks in the neighborhood, tours of which are offered daily.

Early settlers to South Philadelphia were primarily from various towns in the province of Genoa in the region of Liguria and helped found the first Italian national parish in the country, St. Mary Magdalen de Pazzi, which is featured prominently in this volume. Later immigrants from southern Italy mainly consisted of three groups: people from towns in the province of Messina, on the island of Sicily, from the region of Abruzzo, and a large number of people from the provinces of Salerno and Avellino in the region of Campania. Southern Italians founded La Chiesa Nostra Signora del Buon Consiglio—Our Lady of Good Counsel Church—in 1898 because they felt unwelcomed at the predominately Irish St. Peter's and equally unwanted at St. Mary's because they were from the south. The church's constant activity is legendary to this day. South Philadelphia–born Fr. Michael Gambone was quoted in Murray Dubin's 1996 book, *South Philadelphia: Mummers, Memories, and the Melrose Diner*, as saying, "In the 35 years . . . that parish was in existence . . . there were more baptisms than there were at St. Paul in 150 years. . . . One Sunday, there were 84 baptisms . . . Average that out." But, despite the parish's constant activity, the Archdiocese of Philadelphia decided to close it in 1933, amid much controversy. Other Italian national parishes were St. Nicholas of Tolentine, St. Rita of Cascia (now a shrine), and King of Peace, among others.

The Catholic Church is a constant theme in this volume, and for good reason: Italy and Catholicism go hand in hand. Italians practiced Catholicism radically different than the rigid authoritarian Catholic archdiocesan-ruled machine already in place in the city by the time the Italians arrived. The Italian Catholic style of liturgical worship, while centering around the normally prescribed daily and Sunday masses, relied a great deal on processions, popular devotions to patron saints, and a great use of sacramentals, relics, popular imagery, and religious iconography, with a heavy emphases on the public display of worship, as opposed to the more constrained and reserved method of Irish liturgical practice that took place almost entirely within the walls of the parish church with strict attention to diocesan and canon law. This put both groups at odds almost immediately, to say nothing of the linguistic issue compounding the situation even more, since almost none of the Italian immigrants had a working knowledge of English when they came to the United States. Volumes could be written about this alone, not only in Philadelphia but in every other area of the country.

The church was the focal point of neighborhood life. Nearly everything, from baptisms to funerals, played out in or around the church.

But it must also be noted that there existed small groups of Italian Protestants in the city. The Presbyterian Church established three Italian missions in the city (its first in South Philadelphia, its second in Overbrook, and another Italian-language mission in Germantown). There were also Italian Baptists, Pentecostals, evangelicals, and so on. But due to the quick rate of assimilation, the second and third generations moved out of the neighborhood much quicker than Catholics did.

Whenever the public thinks of Italians in Philadelphia, South Philadelphia automatically comes to mind. Indeed, that was the oldest and largest settlement of Italians in the city (and the number of photographs in this book will attest to that), but the other Italian neighborhoods of the city must be appropriately acknowledged and given their due.

Germantown, located in the northwest section of the city, had Italian immigrants settling there as early as 1880. Germantown Italians were a very active and vibrant community and are fiercely proud of who they are to this day. Through a project sponsored by the Germantown Historical Society, and funded by the Pennsylvania Humanities Council, folklorist Dr. Joan L. Saverino studied the migration patterns of Italians to both Germantown and Chestnut Hill. Saverino, through the help of former residents, identified the earliest families to settle in Germantown and Chestnut Hill and approximately when and where. (In Germantown, it all started on the now-defunct Ely Street and on the 500 block of East Rittenhouse Street).

Though nowhere near the numbers of South Philadelphia, Germantown, nonetheless, had its share of noteworthy individuals, such as ballet and dance instructor Emidio (William) Sena; maestro Luigi Giorno, leader of the famed Germantown Community Band; noted folksinger Gina Ventresca Carano, who married prominent Philadelphia attorney Frank Carano (of Overbrook); the Di Pasquale family, a family of musical prodigies who all played in the Philadelphia Orchestra; Cav. Ernesto M. Strollo, his daughter Joanne Strollo, the first, and to date only, female national president in the 101-plus-year history of the Order Sons of Italy in America; Sr. Francis Joseph (Rachael Scarpello), retired mother superior of the religious order of Sisters of the Assumption; noted stained glass maker Nicola D'Ascenzo; the late funeral director Victor J. Errichetti, appointed by the Italian consulate as its official representative in the 1970s for Pennsylvania and New York (a rare honor); photojournalist Mary D'Agostino Nocella, who worked for both the now-defunct *Evening Bulletin* and the *Inquirer* newspapers and traveled extensively throughout Europe, reporting on cultural landmarks all over Europe for those newspapers, and the wife of noted photographer Sam Nocella; Carmella Silvestri Rizzo, wife of the late mayor Frank Lazarro Rizzo and mother of current councilman-at-large Frank Rizzo; the late Judge Tullio Leomporra; and Italian American novelist and journalist Marion Benasuti, author of *No Steady Job for Papa* and other lighthearted novels of an Italian American nature, among many others.

The Germantown settlement is 98 percent gone today, but it never left the hearts and minds of those who lived there in its heyday.

The histories of the Italians of Manayunk and East Falls are topics that deserve to be studied in-depth, as very little information exists on these small, yet proud settlements.

Many Italian-owned businesses still exist in Chestnut Hill to this day. It can also boast notable personalities such as writer David Contosta, among many others. East Falls can also boast of prominent people such as the late Dr. Alma Morani, daughter of a Calabria-born sculptor, who went on to become one of the nation's most prominent plastic surgeons and a foremost authority on facial reconstruction.

The history of the settlements of Frankford and Tacony, in the northeast section of the city, share common elements (Fr. Alfredo Procopio and Fr. James Rosica, among others).

Although the Italian settlement of Frankford is gone now, the people remain proud of their roots and are very open about sharing their memories with people who take the time to ask.

A sorely underrated neighborhood when it comes to Italians is Tacony. There is a small, yet active Little Italy there. There are two Italian funeral homes that remain today, located on the same block (Sanutti and Galzerano, the latter of which used to be the Nicastro Funeral Home, originally of the North Philadelphia settlement of Twenty-second Street), Italian-themed restaurants and cafés, and the national parish Our Lady of Consolation.

Port Richmond continues to thrive with Mother of Divine Grace parish, an active Sons of Italy lodge, and a settlement of Italian Americans who were born, raised, and will die in Port Richmond.

West Philadelphia was a very active neighborhood in the day. It supported three Italian national parishes at one time—St. Donato, Our Lady of the Angels, and Our Lady of the Rosary, the latter two of which have been closed by the Archdiocese of Philadelphia in the past few years. There remain a few Italian businesses, such as Amoroso Baking Company, Caffe Sportivo Italiano, and Morrone Water Ice, among others.

The settlements of North Philadelphia, centered around Twenty-second and Clearfield Streets and St. Mary of the Eternal parish, and Our Lady of Pompeii, centered around Sixth Street and Erie Avenue, are completely gone. Not much information exists about these settlements, and recognition of these enclaves is long overdue.

Italians contributed in so many ways to every facet of Philadelphia life. They labored on the world-famous city hall, Reading Terminal Market, and the subway systems of the Market-Frankford Elevated and Broad Street subway systems of public transit agency Southeastern Pennsylvania Transportation Authority. The way of eating their ancestors have enjoyed for thousands of years, once ridiculed, is now considered to be one of the healthiest in the world, and, most importantly, they made a new life in a country that was radically different from the one they left behind.

The initial exodus of southern Italians in the 1870s and 1880s went to Brazil (São Paulo) and Argentina (Buenos Aires). When the United States became the promised land, southern Italians came to its shores in such large numbers that only Germany sent more immigrants to this country (although it is important to remember that the largest number of Italian immigrants went to Brazil, where there remains to this day the largest number of Italians outside Italy itself). Italians chose to settle primarily in the inner cities of the United States due to the abundance of jobs. Of those cities, New York City was the choice of destination for those immigrants. And although Philadelphia had less than half the number of immigrants New York City saw, it, nonetheless, was the second-most-populous city when it came to Italians.

There is so much to include in a subject of this nature that it is literally impossible to even begin to scratch the surface. With this volume, I have attempted to add something noteworthy to the varied body of work that already exists on this topic. All errors are mine.

One

THE ITALIANS OF SOUTH PHILADELPHIA AND CENTER CITY

South Philadelphia was the oldest and largest Italian settlement in the city. Italians settled there beginning in Colonial times. These early Italians were from northern Italy, and the majority of them were from a variety of cities in the province of Genoa in the region of Liguria. They were sought after for their musical and artistic talents. These northerners also helped to establish the first parish in the country designed specifically to administer to the unique needs of an immigrant community—a national parish. Located at what is now 712 Montrose Street, St. Mary Magdalen de Pazzi was founded in 1852. The parish was a hallmark of the neighborhood and touched many a South Philadelphia Italian's and Italian American's life in one way or another for generations. It was a cultural landmark and is fondly remembered and discussed to this day. Richard N. Juliani, professor of sociology at Villanova University, thoroughly documented every aspect of the Colonial and early-Victorian Italian settlement in his 1998 book, *Building Little Italy: Philadelphia's Italians Before Mass Migration*, which is a must-read.

After the 1861 unification of Italy, South Philadelphia became the destination to waves of southern Italian immigrants. Today the descendents of those southern Italians are synonymous with South Philadelphia—local and world-famous celebrities such as Mario Lanza, Bobby Rydell, Jerry Blavat, and Fabian, scores of judges and politicians including Philadelphia City Council president Anna Cibotti Verna (the first woman and Italian American to hold that position), the late Frank Lazarro Rizzo (the first Italian American police commissioner and the mayor from 1972 to 1980), and the late Thomas Foglietta (ambassador to Italy during the second Clinton administration), and scores of well-known people from all walks of life.

It would literally take an encyclopedia to just scratch the surface of the plethora of societies, churches (Catholic and Protestant), and businesses that called South Philadelphia home, including the Italian Market, the oldest outdoor market in the country.

Although nowhere near the size it once was, and with a large exodus to southern New Jersey (especially to Washington Township), today many Italian Americans still call the South Philadelphia row homes their grandparents and great-grandparents proudly bought home. They continue to make their neighborhood a viable place to live and work.

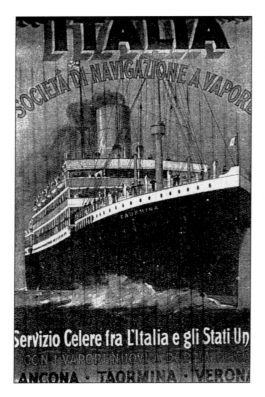

This advertisement for the Italian Steamship Navigation Society offers "celebrated service" from Italy to the United States and highlights the ports of Ancona, Taormina, and Verona. (Courtesy of Celeste A. Morello.)

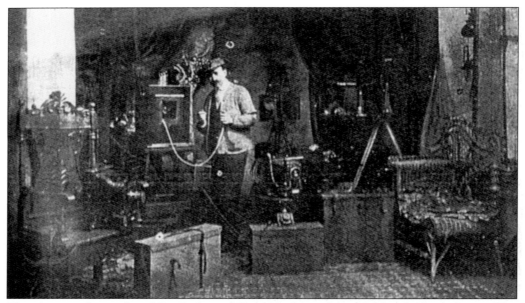

The photography studio of De Carlo and Sons was located on 804 South Ninth Street. The father started his photography business in 1847 and shows off the latest photographic equipment here. (Courtesy of Celeste A. Morello.)

De Laurentis and Teti, located at 766 South Ninth Street, is seen here in 1904. Like the numerous banks located in South Philadelphia in the early 1900s, it offered a variety of services to the Italian immigrant, including telegraphic services, foreign money exchanges, notary services, and steamship tickets to and from Italy. (Courtesy of Celeste A. Morello.)

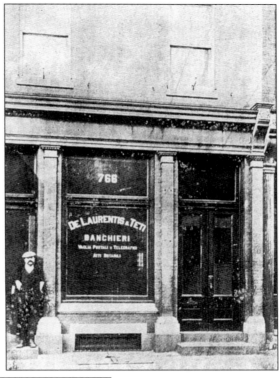

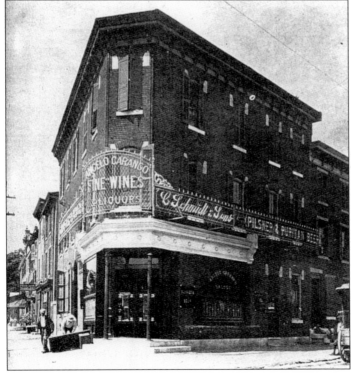

Angelo Carango's store opened on April 13, 1911, in the heart of Little Italy and sold a wide variety of liquors and beers. (Courtesy of Celeste A. Morello.)

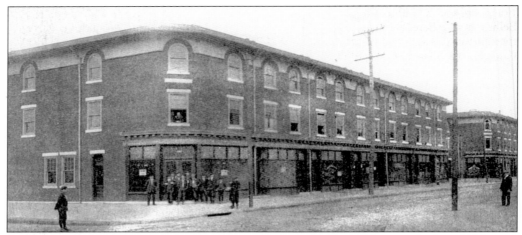

Pictured here is Eighth Street and Washington Avenue. G. Tumolillo owned a lot of 45 houses that were built with modern conveniences. He was a very successful businessman in the city in the early 1900s. (Courtesy of Celeste A. Morello.)

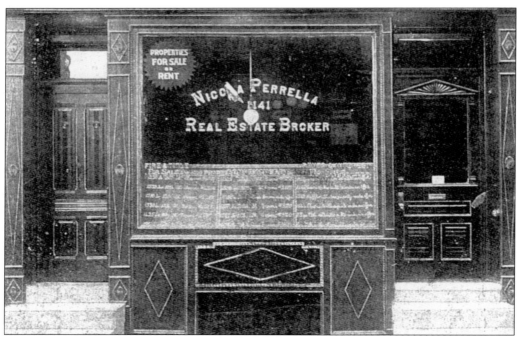

This advertisement for Nicola Perrella's real estate office boasted of a large clientele. He opened his business in 1907. (Courtesy of Celeste A. Morello.)

The photography studio of V. S. Bellino is seen here. He was a specialist in the use of flashlight. (Courtesy of Celeste A. Morello.)

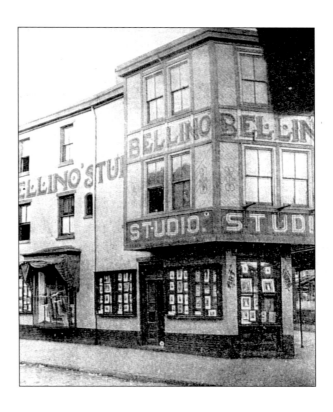

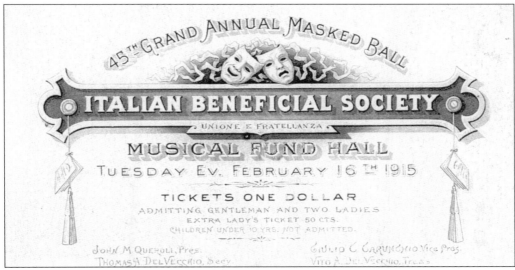

This card announces a masked ball for the Italian Beneficial Society. The masks and the timing of the ball, the middle of February, suggest a highbrow celebration of Fat Tuesday, the day before the start of Lent where Catholics are asked to fast and sacrifice. Carnival, the largest celebrations of which are hosted by Brazil, began in Venice in medieval times. (Courtesy of Celeste A. Morello.)

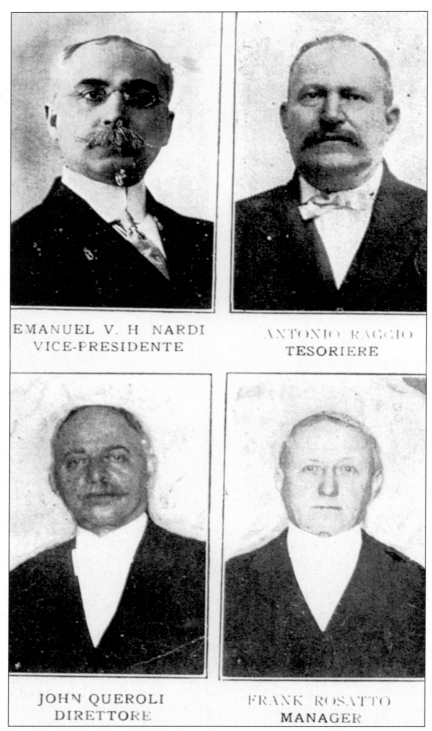

EMANUEL V. H NARDI
VICE-PRESIDENTE

ANTONIO RAGGIO
TESORIERE

JOHN QUEROLI
DIRETTORE

FRANK ROSATTO
MANAGER

The officers of the Italian Beneficial Society whose names appear on the announcement for the masked ball are pictured here. (Courtesy of Celeste A. Morello.)

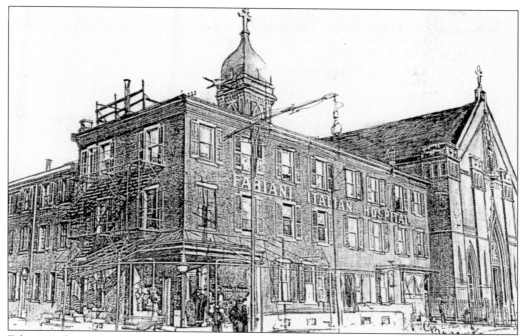

Fabiani Italian Hospital was located in the heart of Little Italy and was one block from the Ninth Street Italian Market. It was right next to St. Paul's Church (located at the right-hand side of this drawing). It served the Little Italy community for many years. (Courtesy of Celeste A. Morello.)

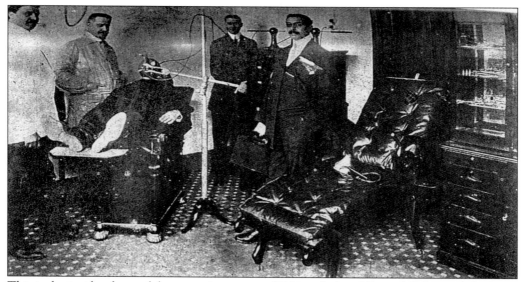

This is the inside of one of the operating rooms of Fabiani Italian Hospital. It boasted the latest in medical technology and techniques: top-of-the-line X-ray machines diagnosing fractures, dislocated bones, and tumors. The hospital also cured diseases of the blood and skin. (Courtesy of Celeste A. Morello.)

OSPEDALE ITALIANO FABIANI

L'OSPEDALE FABIANI, DIRETTO, CON

FEDE D'APOSTOLO, DAL DR. GIUSEPPE FA-

BIANI, SI E' TRASFERITO NEL MONUMENTA-

LE FABBRICATO MESSO SU CON GUSTO ED

ELEGANZA, AL

S. W. COR. 10th & CARPENTER STREETS

DIPARTIMENTI

MEDICO-CHIRURGICO, OCCHI, NASO, ORECCHI E GO-
LA, GENITO-URINARIO, MALATTIE DELLE
DONNE, Dentistico, Elettrici a'. Ragg: N. Iniezioni 606, **Farmacia**

☞ **OPERAZIONI** ☜

**Gli ammalati vengono operati senza ad
mentarsi e senza dolore**

Essi possono mangiare, bere, parlare, leggere, fumare, ecc., duran-
te l'operazione. Il Dr. Fabiani esce per visitare gli ammalati a casa.

This advertisement for Fabiani Italian Hospital appeared in the February 5, 1927, edition of *La Libera Parola* (the free word), one of several Italian-language newspapers in Philadelphia that served Italian immigrants of the entire city.

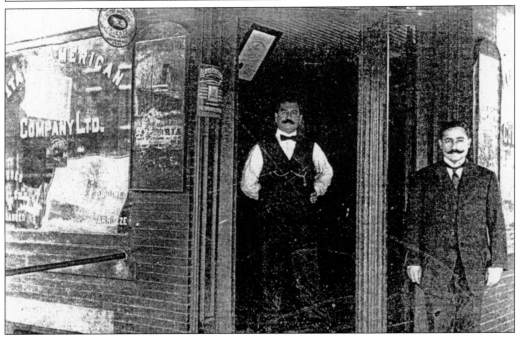

The Italo-American Company, Ltd., was founded in 1905 and was located on the northwest corner of Ninth and Christian Streets, in the very heart of Little Italy. It was the successor to the Italo-American Trust Company, founded in 1902. (Courtesy of Celeste A. Morello.)

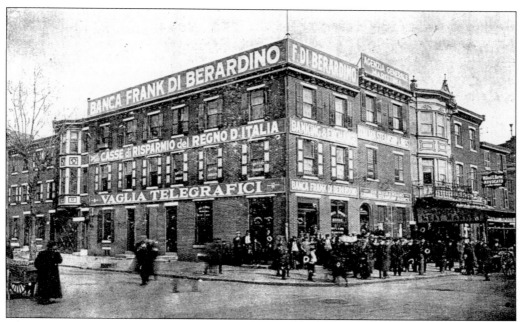

This is the Bank of Frank Di Berardino at 821 Christian Street. His was one of numerous independent banks throughout South Philadelphia that offered a variety of services for Italian immigrants to communicate with their families who were still in Italy. (Courtesy of Celeste A. Morello.)

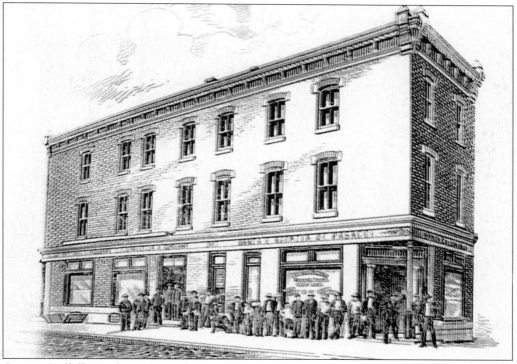

Cerceo-Ciallella Bank was located at 700 Christian Street. (Courtesy of Celeste A. Morello.)

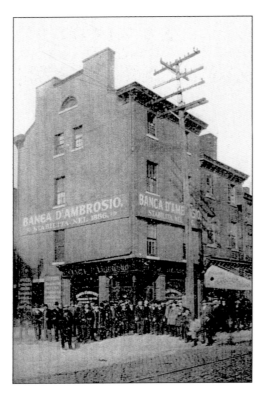

The D'Ambrosio Bank was the first Italian bank in South Philadelphia, opening in 1886. Besides dealing with money, it issued steamship tickets to and from Italy, as later banks would do, dealt in real estate, and also served as an employment agency for immigrants. Bank owner Harry D'Ambrosio claimed to send as many as 10,000 immigrant workers to area employers in 1902. (Courtesy of Celeste A. Morello.)

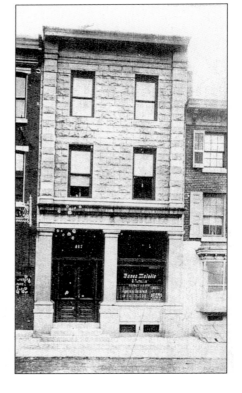

Maiella Bank, operated by Giorgio Tumolillo, was founded in 1887 and also had a branch at 30 Piazza della Borsa in Naples. The bank may have existed for 50 years. (Courtesy of Celeste A. Morello.)

This advertisement for the bank of Charles C. A. (Carmine Antonio) Baldi and Brothers appeared in the July 29, 1927, edition of *L'Opinione* (the opinion). Baldi was born in Castelnuovo Cliento, Salerno, Campania, and immigrated to the United States when he was 14. He established himself in a variety of diverse endeavors. He was the first Italian elected to the Philadelphia school board. The C. C. A. Baldi Middle School at 8801 Verree Road in Northeast Philadelphia is named for him.

AVVISO
AI POSSESSORI DEL
SECOND LIBERTY LOAN BONDS

I SECOND LIBERTY BONDS saranno redimibili dal 15 Novembre 1926 e gli interessi cesseranno da quella data.

I Bonds devono presentarsi il 15 Novembre 1927 ad una Federal Reserve Bank.
Noi vi assisteremo nell'ottenere il rimborso.

IMPORTANTE

Prima del 15 Novembre 1927 il Segretario del Tesoro può estendere il privilegio ai possessori dei Second Liberty Loan Bonds di cambiare questi per altre sicurtà del Governo degli Stati Uniti.

Venite da noi e vi daremo ogni spiegazione al riguardo

FIRST ITALIAN EXCHANGE BANK
CHARLES C. A. BALDI & BROS.

928 So. 8th Street Philadelphia, Pa.

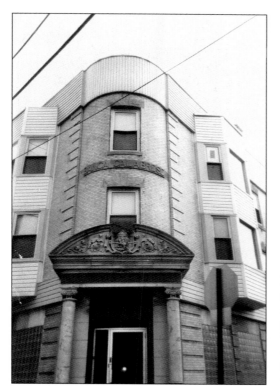

Banca Calabrese was located at Sixth and Christian Streets. Many banks were established to serve the financial needs of a group of people from a particular region. The bank's location suggests this was where a settlement of immigrants from Calabria settled in South Philadelphia. (Author's collection.)

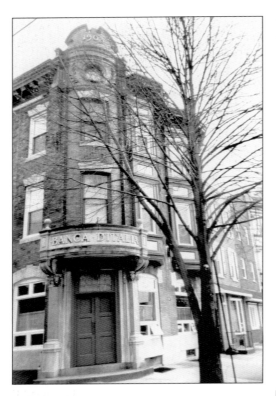

Located just a block from Banca Calabrese was Banca D'Italia at Sixth and Fitzwater Streets. (Author's collection.)

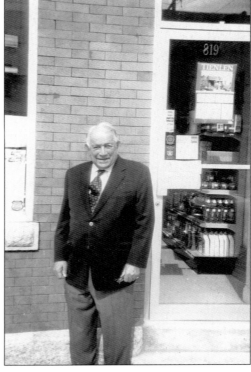

Luke Marano is the chairman of the Philadelphia Macaroni Company. The Marano family is world famous for its numerous varieties of pasta, which can be found in such national products as Progresso, Campbell's Soup, Lipton, Ronzoni, and Marie Callender TV dinners, among many others. His grandfather Antonio started the business, and today he runs the business with his sons. (Author's collection.)

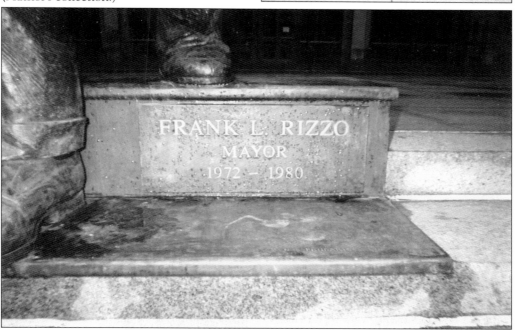

Frank Lazarro Rizzo (1920–1991) was born in South Philadelphia and rose through the ranks of city government starting as a city policeman and eventually becoming both the first Italian American police commissioner and mayor, to which he was elected in 1972. He died in 1991 during another run for mayor. This statue is located outside the Municipal Services Building at 1401 JFK Boulevard in Center City. (Author's collection.)

FRANK L. RIZZO
MAYOR
1972 – 1980

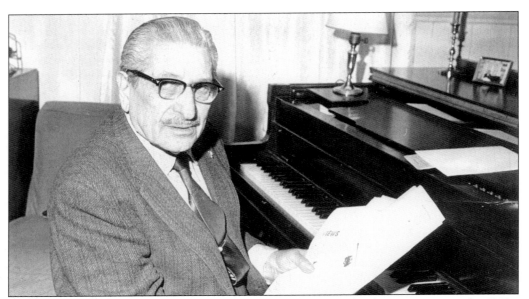

Naples-born Ralph Borrelli was a very popular and much-beloved radio announcer in the 1930s, 1940s, and 1950s. He was the host of an Italian-language variety show on WRAX-AM (which later merged with WPEN-AM). Local Italians called it "Borelli's station." Philadelphia had a few Italian-language radio programs, another of which was hosted by Frank Trombetta, born in Catanzaro, Calabria. He had a program on WTEL and was a well-known mandolinist. (Courtesy of Temple University Libraries, Urban Archives.)

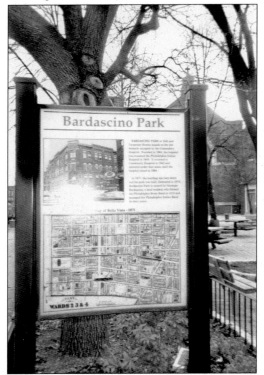

Bardascino Park, located at Tenth and Carpenter Streets, lays on the site of the Community Hospital, founded in 1904. The name was changed to Philadelphia Italian Hospital in 1936, but reverted to its original name in 1942. The building was demolished in 1977. The park is named after Giuseppe Bardascino, maestro of the Philadelphia Brass Band and manager of the Philadelphia Italian Band for 40 years. (Author's collection.)

The performance hall of the Giannini family, which was a famous music family, is seen here. Patriarch Ferruccio was the first person to sing on a record, daughter Dusolina was a world-famous soprano, son Vittorio was an accomplished composer and music teacher, and mother Antoinetta was a gifted violinist. (Courtesy of Celeste A. Morello.)

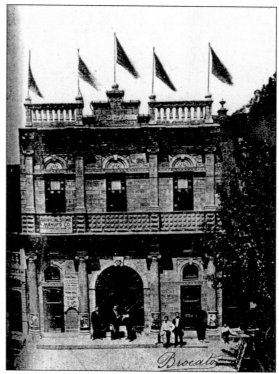

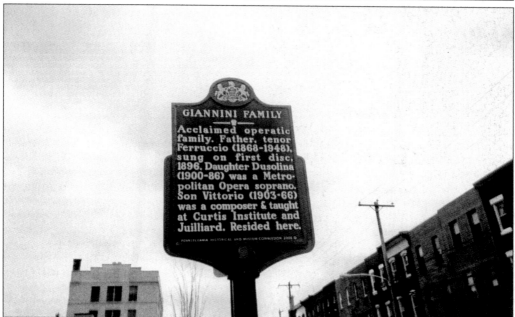

A marker is the highest form of recognition the Commonwealth of Pennsylvania bestows on an individual or establishment. People who are nominated for a marker must be deceased. This marker for the Giannini family is placed near the site of the family's residence at 727 Christian Street. (Courtesy of the Pennsylvania Historical and Museum Commission.)

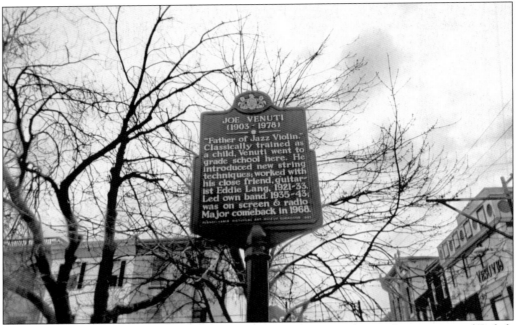

This is the state historical marker for jazz pioneer Joe Venuti at the northeast corner of Eighth and Fitzwater Streets. (Courtesy of the Pennsylvania Historical and Museum Commission.)

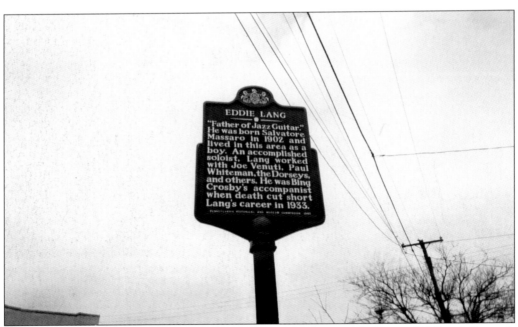

This is the state historical marker for Eddie Lang, born Salvatore Massaro at 748 South Seventh Street. He had a distinguished career in jazz alongside childhood friend Joe Venuti. He died in New York City in late March 1933 at the age of 30 after an operation to remove his tonsils. (Courtesy of the Pennsylvania Historical and Museum Commission.)

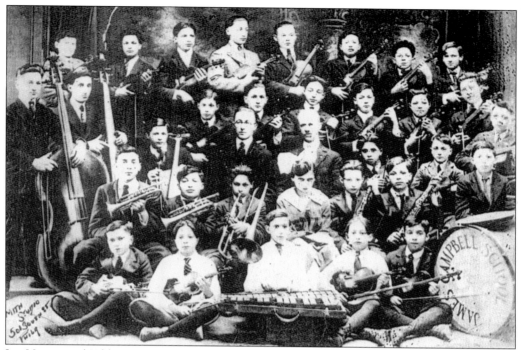

Joe Venuti and Eddie Lang appear in a *c.* 1912 group photograph of neighborhood child music prodigies. (Courtesy of Celeste A. Morello.)

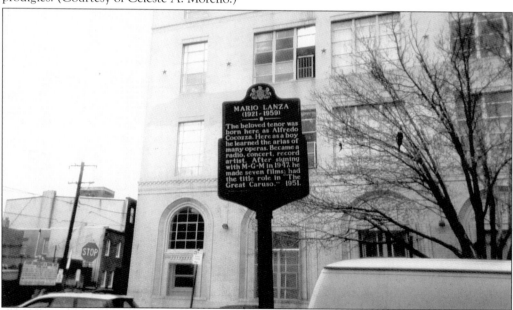

This is the state historical marker for world-famous tenor Mario Lanza at Sixth and Christian Streets. Born Alfredo Cocozza, he led a distinguished musical career to which present-day tenors find themselves constantly compared. He attended South Philadelphia High School and first sang "Ave Maria" at St. Mary Magdalen de Pazzi Church. He took his mother's maiden name as his stage name. (Courtesy of the Pennsylvania Historical and Museum Commission.)

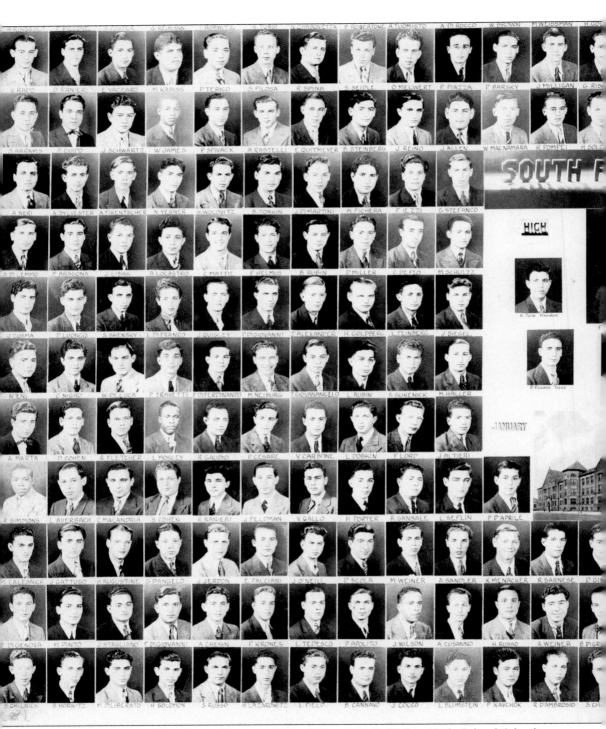

This is picture of the class of January 1939 of South Philadelphia High School (also known as Southern High). Many Italian immigrants sent their children to public schools due to the rigid authoritarianism of American Catholic schools. Though those children attended public

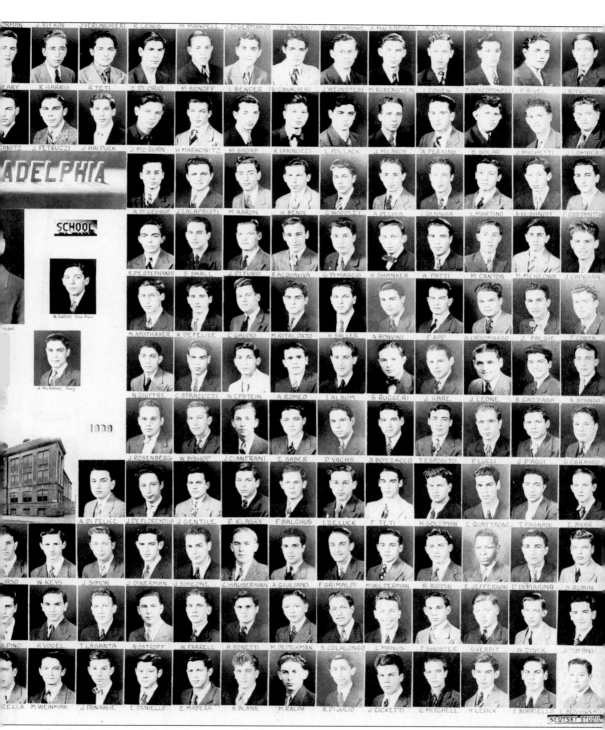

schools, they attended Confraternity of Christian Doctrine (CCD) classes at the neighborhood Catholic school in order to receive the sacraments and, later on, be married in a Catholic church. (Courtesy of Norman Giorno-Calapristi.)

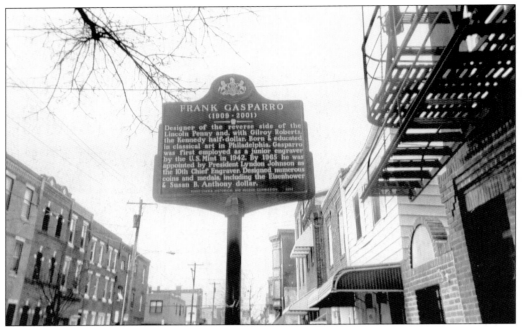

This is the state historical marker for Frank Gasparro, designer of the Lincoln penny and Kennedy half-dollar, among other coins. (Courtesy of the Pennsylvania Historical and Museum Commission.)

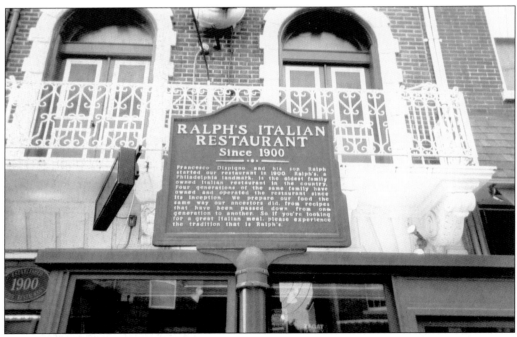

A privately issued marker stands outside of Ralph's Italian Restaurant, "the oldest family-owned Italian restaurant in the country," which has been a neighborhood fixture for over a century. The restaurant is located on Ninth Street near Catharine Street. (Author's collection.)

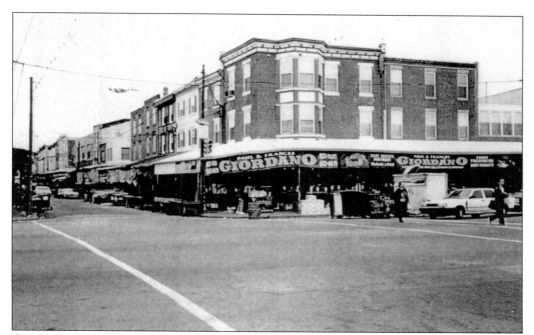

Giordano's, at Ninth Street and Washington Avenue, in the heart of the Italian Market, has operated for over 75 years. The Italian Market is the oldest continually run outdoor market in the country. (Courtesy of Celeste A. Morello.)

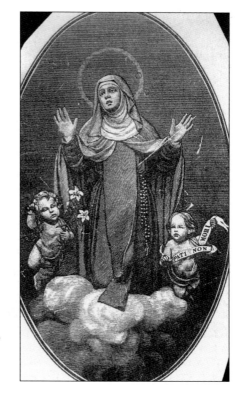

St. Mary Magdalen de Pazzi was born on April 5, 1566, in Florence and baptized Caterina. She was a deeply religious woman, entering religious life at age 16 as a Carmelite nun. She died on May 25, 1607, and was canonized by Pope Clement IX on April 28, 1669. Her feast day is May 27, and she is the patron saint against sickness and sexual temptation. (Courtesy of Celeste A. Morello.)

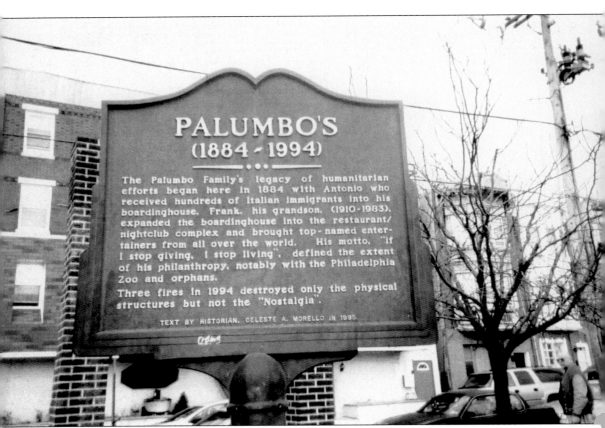

PALUMBO'S
(1884 ~ 1994)

The Palumbo Family's legacy of humanitarian efforts began here in 1884 with Antonio who received hundreds of Italian immigrants into his boardinghouse. Frank, his grandson, (1910-1983), expanded the boardinghouse into the restaurant/nightclub complex and brought top-named entertainers from all over the world. His motto, "if I stop giving, I stop living", defined the extent of his philanthropy, notably with the Philadelphia Zoo and orphans.

Three fires in 1994 destroyed only the physical structures but not the "Nostalgia".

TEXT BY HISTORIAN, CELESTE A. MORELLO IN 1995.

Palumbo's originally started as a boardinghouse for immigrants from the region of Abruzzo. The house eventually became home to one of the most celebrated landmarks in Philadelphia history, with the establishment of a restaurant and nightclub where numerous celebrities went to see and be seen. A series of fires in the summer of 1994 gutted the building, and it was decided by the family to let Palumbo's live on in spirit. (Author's collection.)

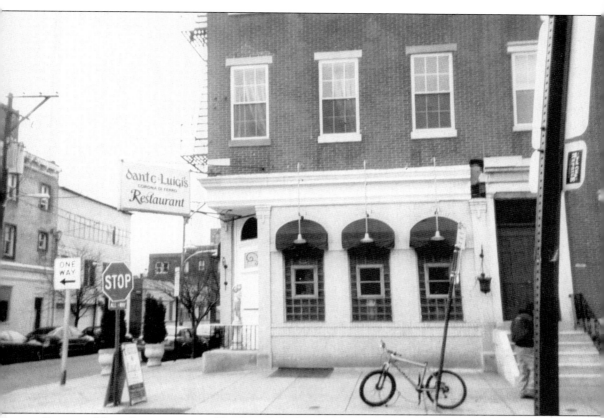

Dante and Luigi's restaurant, at Tenth and Catharine Streets, has been a neighborhood fixture since 1899. (Author's collection.)

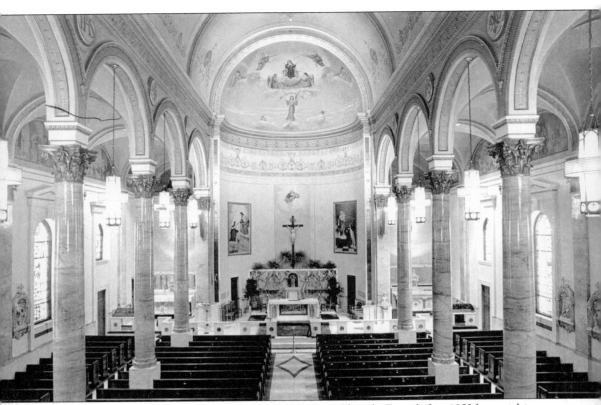

Seen here is the interior of St. Mary Magdalen de Pazzi Church. Founded in 1852 by parishioners from the province of Genoa in the region of Liguria in northern Italy, it was the oldest Italian national parish in the United States. It was suppressed as a parish on July 1, 2000, by the Archdiocese of Philadelphia. (Courtesy of Temple University Libraries, Urban Archives.)

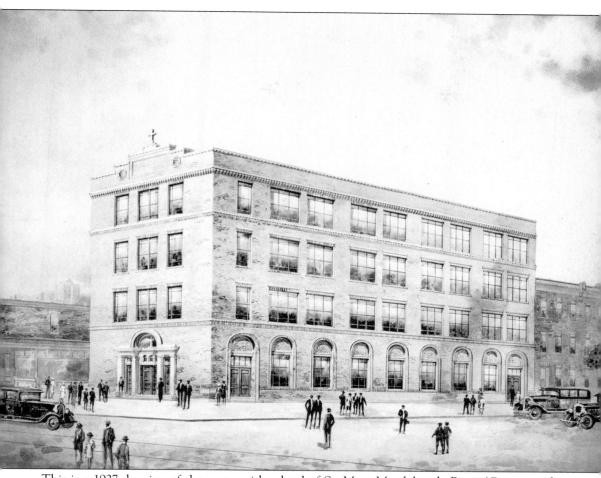

This is a 1927 drawing of the new parish school of St. Mary Magdalen de Pazzi. (Courtesy of Temple University Libraries, Urban Archives.)

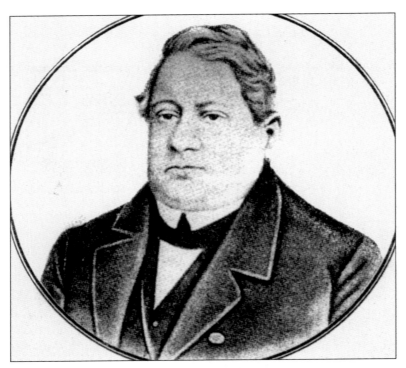

Fr. Gaetano Mariani was the first pastor of St. Mary's. He was born in Florence and came to the United States in 1851. He was a music teacher at St. Charles Borromeo Seminary before being assigned as the pastor for the new (and first) Italian national parish in South Philadelphia. (Courtesy of Celeste A. Morello.)

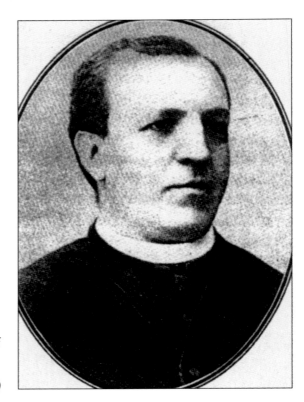

Fr. Antonio Isoleri was an early pastor of St. Mary's. He is seen here from a 1952 book celebrating the centennial of the parish. (Courtesy of Celeste A. Morello.)

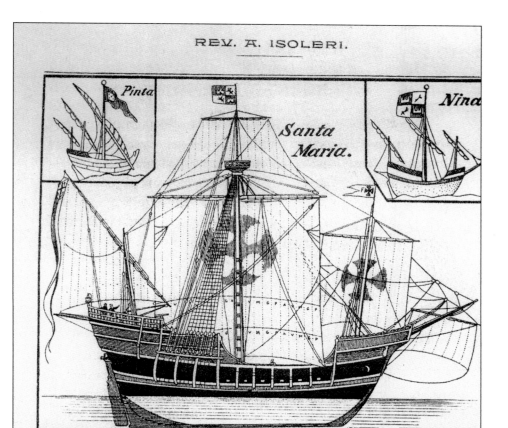

REV. A. ISOLERI.

Pinta

Santa Maria.

Nina

[Reproduced from American Ecclesiastical Review, October, 1892.]
(LE TRE CARAVELLE.)

✳ UN RICORDO ✳

DELLE

FESTE COLOMBIANE,

CELEBRATE IN PHILADELPHIA, STATI UNITI D' AMERICA,
NELL' OTTOBRE DEL 1892.

PHILADELPHIA:
PENN PRINTING HOUSE, 123 SOUTH ELEVENTH ST.
1893.

A Remembrance of the Columbian Festivities

Father Isoleri was born near Genoa and wrote a book in 1892 to commemorate the 400th anniversary of Christopher Columbus's voyage to the New World. (Courtesy of Celeste A. Morello.)

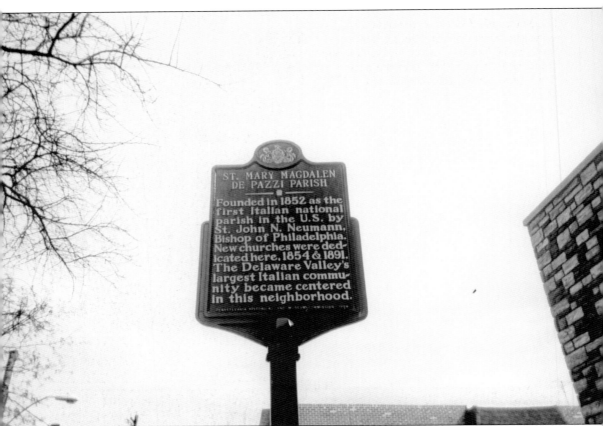

Seen here is the state historical marker for St. Mary's. It is located in front of the church itself at 712 Montrose Street and commemorates its status as the oldest Italian national parish in the country as well as South Philadelphia's status as the largest Italian settlement in the area. (Courtesy of the Pennsylvania Historical and Museum Commission.)

The Madonna House, located directly across the street from St. Paul's Church at Tenth and Christian Streets, housed Mother Cabrini's Missionary Sisters of the Sacred Heart, an order of nuns she founded in 1880. (Author's collection.)

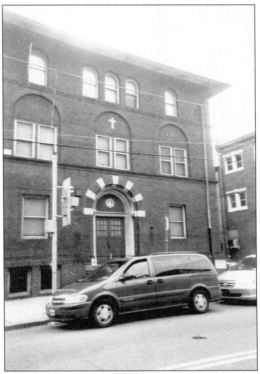

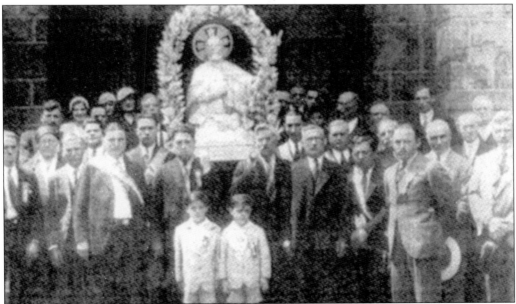

Seen here is the 1932 procession of Our Lady of Good Counsel Church. Established in 1898 at 816 Christian Street, it was the parish of choice for southern Italian immigrants who felt unwelcome both at the predominately Irish St. Paul's and at the northern Italian stronghold of St. Mary's. It was one of the most active parishes in Philadelphia history. Despite this, the church was closed in 1933 amid much controversy and protest. (Courtesy of Celeste A. Morello.)

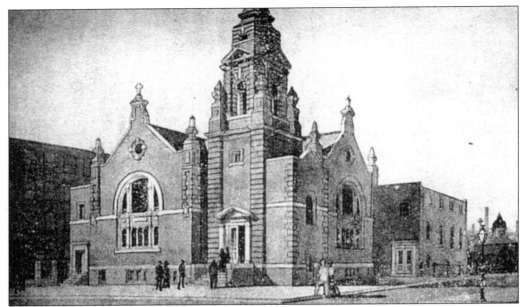

The First Italian Presbyterian Church's first services were held under a tent near Tenth and Carpenter Streets. It quickly had enough members to purchase a lot and build a new church near the site of the tent prayer services. Protestant missions made a special outreach to Italian immigrants to speed up the assimilation process. As a result, some Italian immigrants became Presbyterians, Baptists, and Methodists, among other denominations. (Courtesy of Celeste A. Morello.)

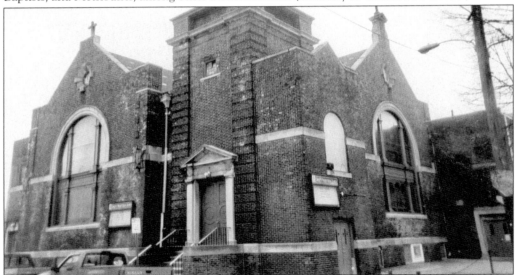

The First Italian Presbyterian Church was located at Tenth and Carpenter Streets. In an effort to attract Italian immigrants, Protestant denominations set up missions in various Italian neighborhoods. The Presbyterian Church formally established its first Italian mission in 1903 in South Philadelphia. This building could seat 1,200 people, and the congregation flourished for 20 years. Due to the quick rate of assimilation, the children and grandchildren of immigrants moved from the neighborhood. Today the church serves a predominately Vietnamese and Indonesian congregation. (Author's collection.)

Shown here is the exterior of St. Rita's Church, located at Broad and Ellsworth Streets. Like St. Nicholas of Tolentine, St. Rita's was established in 1907. Today it serves as the National Shrine to St. Rita. (Courtesy of Temple University Libraries, Urban Archives.)

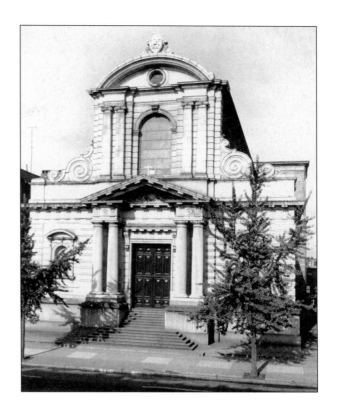

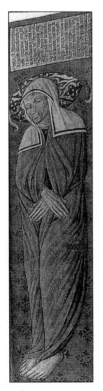

St. Rita of Cascia was born Rita Lotti in 1381 in Roccaporena, Cascia, Umbria, and died on May 22, 1457. Her body, which has not decayed in over 500 years, is displayed under a glass case in the basilica of her namesake church in Cascia. Visitors have reported throughout the years of seeing the body in different positions under the glass case and of her eyes opening and closing unaided. (Courtesy of Celeste A. Morello.)

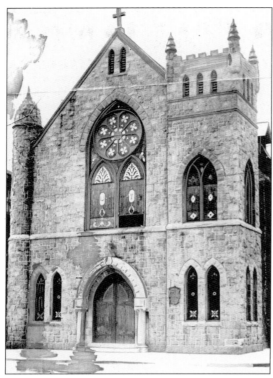

St. Nicholas of Tolentine Church, located at Ninth and Watkins Streets, is seen here in 1912. The church's patron, Augustinian monk Nicholas Gurruti, was born in Sant'Angelo, Potano, Marche, Italy, in 1245. The parish continues to assist present-day Italian immigrants with the many aspects of adjusting to life in a new country. (Courtesy of Temple University Libraries, Urban Archives.)

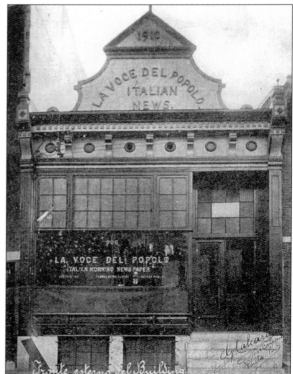

Pictured here is the office of the Italian-language daily newspaper *La Voce del Popolo* (the voice of the people). It commenced publication on May 20, 1906. (Courtesy of Celeste A. Morello.)

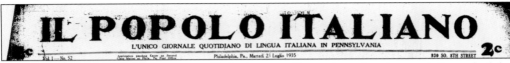

IL POPOLO ITALIANO

L'UNICO GIORNALE QUOTIDIANO DI LINGUA ITALIANA IN PENNSYLVANIA

Vol. I — No. 52 Philadelphia, Pa., Martedì 23 Luglio 1935 930 SO. 8TH STREET 2c

Italian-language publications were established in an effort to keep immigrants informed of the goings on in their native country as well as to understand what was going on in their adopted country. *Il Popolo Italiano* (the Italian people) and *L'Opinione* (the opinion), published by Charles C. A. Baldi, were two such newspapers to keep immigrants up-to-date on current events. Both newspapers were published in South Philadelphia. The first Italian-language newspaper in the city was *La Gazzetta Italiana* (the Italian gazette), published in the early 1850s.

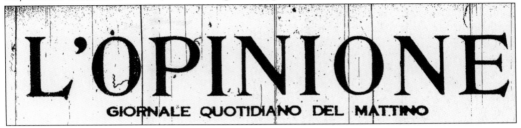

L'OPINIONE

GIORNALE QUOTIDIANO DEL MATTINO

LA LIBERA PAROLA

ITALIAN WEEKLY NEWSPAPER
WITH THE LARGEST CIRCULATION

I forti caratteri sono gli Dei Supremi della Storia Nazionale

Fa quel che devi, avvenga che può

Cav. Uff. A: GIUSEPPE DI SILVESTRO, Direttore
1505-07 So. 15th Street

AVANTI SEMPRE CON LA FIACCOLA IN PUGNO
"Entered as second-class matter April 19th, 1918, at the Post Office at Philadelphia, Pa., under the Act of March 3rd, 1879"

ABBONAMENTO ANNUO $2.00

La Libera Parola (the free word) was also published in South Philadelphia by Giuseppe De Silvestro. *Ordine Nuovo* (new order) was the Italian-language newspaper of the Order Sons of Italy in America (OSIA). There was a small section of the newspaper written in English. In the present day, its monthly newspaper has a small section written in Italian as the language was not passed on to the second and third generations.

Ordine Nuovo
N E W   O R D E R
A Weekly Newspaper Devoted to the Interest of the Italo-Americans of Pennsylvania
OFFICIAL ORGAN OF THE GRAND LODGE OF PENNSYLVANIA
ORDER SONS OF ITALY IN AMERICA

South Philadelphia was host to a slew of Italian funeral homes. Baldi, Verna, Monti-Rago, and Ingenito are some recognizable names to South Philadelphia natives. The Italian Burial Casket Company was run by the Jacovini family. This advertisement ran in the December 21, 1929, edition of *La Libera Parola*.

Termini Brothers Bakery was one of many bakeries in South Philadelphia that created Italian confections that gave immigrants a taste of the Old World in their new surroundings. Among other prominent bakeries in South Philadelphia were La Rosa on Passyunk Avenue and Isgro at Tenth and Christian Streets. This advertisement is from *La Libera Parola*, August 23, 1930.

Giovanni Ingenito specialized in voice lessons, and he prepared students for operas and concerts. This advertisement is from *L'Opinione*, July 31, 1927.

Vito Baldi raves about his outstanding service in giving people the best modern funeral money can buy. This appeared in *La Libera Parola* on December 3, 1932.

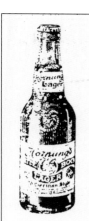

This appeared in *La Libera Parola* on December 10, 1932.

Arnao and Pagano's central warehouse was located at Ninth and Moore Streets in South Philadelphia, but it reached out to the Germantown settlement by stating in this August 23, 1930, advertisement in *La Libera Parola* how useless it was to have to go to South Philadelphia to get what one needed. As a result, a new store was established in Germantown.

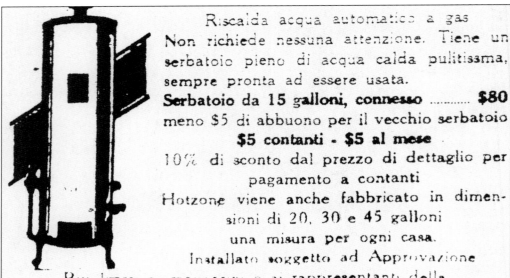

Riscalda acqua automatico a gas
Non richiede nessuna attenzione. Tiene un
serbatoio pieno di acqua calda pulitissma,
sempre pronta ad essere usata.
Serbatoio da 15 galloni, connesso **$80**
meno $5 di abbuono per il vecchio serbatoio
$5 contanti - $5 al mese
10% di sconto dal prezzo di dettaglio per
pagamento a contanti
Hotzone viene anche fabbricato in dimen-
sioni di 20, 30 e 45 galloni
una misura per ogni casa.
Installato soggetto ad Approvazione
Rivolgersi ai magazzini o ai rappresentanti della
The Philadelphia Gas Works Co.

In this advertisement from 1928, the Philadelphia Gas Works suggested people install a hot-water heater in their homes. Notice the English words *hotzone* and *gas* inserted into the advertisement. This was the beginning of incorporating English into Italian to get immigrants to assimilate.

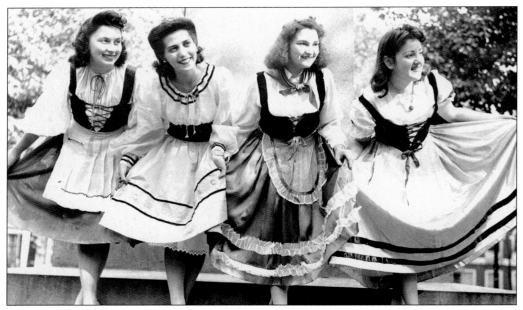

Seen here from left to right are Florence D'Alessandro, Ledena Tonioni, Connie Rainoni, and Ellen Tartaglia in Italian costume at the 1941 Columbus Day parade. The parade is held every year on the first Sunday of October at Marconi Plaza—Broad Street and Oregon Avenue—in South Philadelphia. The parade celebrates the heritage and contributions of Italian Americans both locally and nationally. (Courtesy of Temple University Libraries, Urban Archives.)

DISSOLUTION—The PARTNERSHIP heretofore existing between Giovanni & Oiver, as Fruiterers and Confectioners, is this day DISSOLVED by mutual consent. All persons indebted to said firm are requested to settle with Joseph M Oliver, at No. 248 MARKET Street.

DOMINICO GIOVANNI,
JOSEPH M. OLIVER.

JOSEPH M. OLIVER respectfully informs his friends and the public in general, that he will continue the FRUIT and CONFECTIONERY BUSINESS, at No. 248 MARKET Street, below Eighth, and intends keeping constantly on hand a supply of every thing in that line, which will be sold on the lowest terms possible. jy21-eod3t

This advertisement from the July 24, 1847, issue of the *Public Ledger* demonstrates that Italians from northern Italy ran their own businesses and were successful enough to buy advertisements. Here Joseph M. Oliver (presumably Olivieri) announces the end of his fruit and confectionary stand with Dominico (Domenico) Giovanni at 248 Market Street. Oliver also announces he will continue to operate the stand himself, promising an assortment of goods to be sold at the lowest prices.

Macchinario Elettrico
FORZA ELETTRICA

Riparazioni di Ogni Descrizione
Impianti di Luce e Forza Elettrica

HENRY E. SECHRIST

1217 Race St.   Phila., Pa.

Locust 3835   Race 4372

Non-Italian business owners reached out to the Italian community via Italian-language newspapers. Electrician Henry Sechrist offered his services in repairing all things electrical in this advertisement from the July 7, 1927, edition of *L'Opinione*.

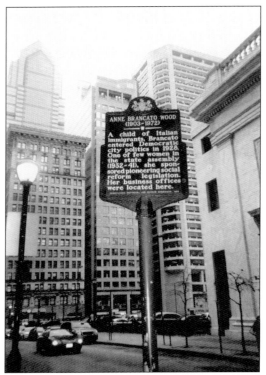

Anne Brancato Wood, a daughter of Italian immigrants, was a real estate broker who rose through the political ranks to become the first woman Democrat elected to the Pennsylvania legislature. In 1935, she became the first woman speaker pro tempore of the House of Representatives in Pennsylvania. This marker stands near the site of her office at Broad and Chestnut Streets in the heart of Center City. (Courtesy of the Pennsylvania Historical and Museum Commission.)

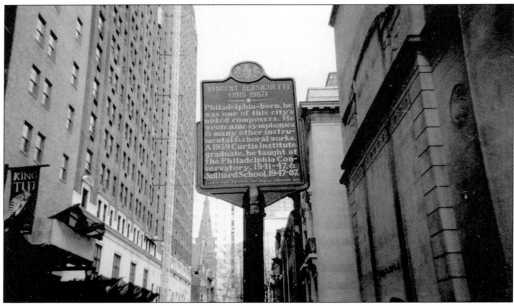

Musical prodigy Vincent Persechetti was born in South Philadelphia. He was involved in every aspect of music. He mastered a variety of wind instruments, taught at the prestigious Julliard School in New York in the 1940s, was a music editor in the early 1950s, and was a prolific and well-respected composer. This marker stands outside the legendary Curtis Institute of Music on Locust Street. (Courtesy of the Pennsylvania Historical and Museum Commission.)

Two

THE ITALIANS OF NORTHWEST PHILADELPHIA

The little-known Italian community of Northwest Philadelphia was, perhaps, the second largest in population behind South Philadelphia. It consisted of the neighborhoods of Germantown, Chestnut Hill, and Mount Airy—remnants of the original German Township prior to its incorporation into the city limits of Philadelphia in 1854, along with the smaller communities of Manayunk and East Falls.

Germantown consisted of two main settlements. Immigrants from Luzzi, Cosenza, Calabria, settled primarily around the now-defunct Ely Street, and another big settlement of immigrants from Palomonte, Salerno, Campania, settled on the 300 block of East Rittenhouse Street, nicknamed the "Yards." There were, of course, immigrants from other regions of Italy who settled in the neighborhood. (Other groups of immigrants from Luzzi settled in Chestnut Hill, East Falls, and Manayunk.)

As in every Philadelphia Italian enclave, life centered around the neighborhood parish. In Germantown, there was Our Lady of the Rosary ("Holy Rosary"), founded in 1894 as the basement chapel at 500 East Chelten Avenue (the upper church was Immaculate Conception). In 1927, a small building that housed an African Methodist Episcopal church at Haines Street and Belfield Avenue was bought and demolished, and a new stone church was erected. Holy Rosary was the Italian national parish for the Italians of Germantown and Chestnut Hill (St. Michael of the Saints served as the parish for the Italian settlement in lower Germantown, dubbed the "Brickyard").

An Italian Protestant mission has its origins at 338 East Rittenhouse Street, beginning in November 1906. By 1929, it was known as La Chiesa Presbyteriana del Salvatore (the Presbyterian Church of the Savior). In February 1960, the church merged with the Market Square Church on Germantown Avenue.

In Chestnut Hill, the two main groups that settled there were from the extremes of Italy. One group was from Luzzi, the other from Poffabro, Udine, Friuli-Venezia Giulia, in the extreme northeast of Italy.

St. Lucy's was the Italian national parish for Manayunk and East Falls. Even though there was a big settlement of Italians in East Falls (primarily from Luzzi and from towns in the province of Campobasso, region of Molise), an Italian parish was never established there. Those Italians attended either St. Bridget's on Midvale Avenue or St. Lucy's.

Page No. Eleven
Supervisor's Dist. No. One
Enumeration Dist. No. 239

Note A.—The Census Year begins June 1, 1879, and ends May 31, 1880.
Note B.—All persons will be included in the Enumeration who were living on the 1st day of June, 1880. No others will. Children BORN SINCE June 1, 1880, will be OMITTED. Members of Families who have DIED SINCE June 1, 1880, will be INCLUDED.
Note C.—Questions Nos. 13, 14, 22 and 23 are not to be asked in respect to persons under 10 years of age.

264

SCHEDULE 1.—Inhabitants in Philadelphia, in the County of Philadelphia, State of Pennsylvania, enumerated by me on the Fourth day of June, 1880.

Jacob N. Drair, Enumerator.

		Name		Place of birth
91	95	Smith, Thomas	W M 50	Ireland
		Roland, James	W M 66	Italy
		Alizeri, Joseph	W M 55	Italy
		Haire, Silvester	W M 38	Ireland
		Hartnett, Jerem.	W M 30	Ireland
		McHale, Patrick	W M 44	Ireland
		Donohue, Will.	W M 42	England
		Shaw, Thomas	W M 43	Missouri
		Smith, August	W M 23	Ireland
		Kennilley, James	W M 29	Canada
		Sullivan, James	W M 25	N Y
		Lissiuque, Victor	W M 24	N Y
		Molas, Wm. B	W M 25	Louisiana
		Hargan, James	W M 26	
		Grant, Richard	W M 27	
		Barre, John	W M 21	

In the 1880 census, two Italian priests, James Rolando and Joseph Alizeri (possibly a corruption of Secundus Lavizeri), were stationed at the "Catholic College of Chelten Avenue," which is St. Vincent's Seminary. Both priests' names appear in St. Vincent's books beginning in 1868. This could suggest the need for Italian-speaking priests as early as 1880 in Germantown. (Courtesy of the National Archives and Records Administration, Mid-Atlantic Region.)

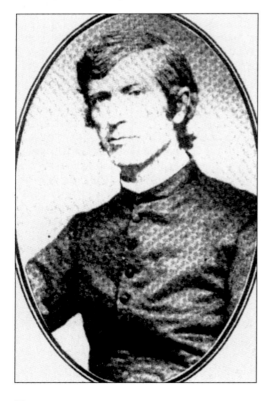

Fr. James Rolando, C.M., appeared in the 1880 census three years prior to his death. He was assigned for a short time as pastor of St. Mary Magdalen de Pazzi in South Philadelphia. (Courtesy of Celeste A. Morello.)

According to the 1880 census, Paul Antoni (likely Paolo Antonio) and his family were found to be living in "the rear of East Chelten Avenue." No definitive street address was given, but he is the only Italian listed in Germantown in the 1880 census. If other Italians were living in Germantown at that time, the census taker did not document them. (Courtesy of the National Archives and Records Administration, Mid-Atlantic Region.)

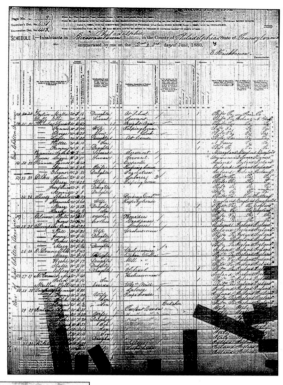

Italian immigrants, regardless of age, willingly signed up for military service during World War I (1914–1918). Many immigrants served with the Italian military, while other immigrants chose to serve in the American military. Joseph (Giuseppe) Di Giacomo, the author's great-grandfather, settled in the Neapolitan enclave of Price and Bayton Streets in Germantown in the early 1900s. (Courtesy of the National Archives and Records Administration, Mid-Atlantic Region.)

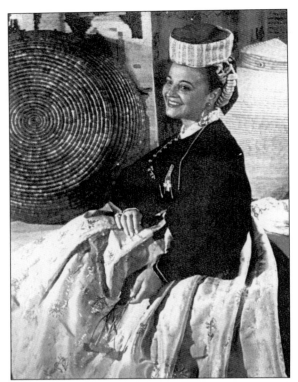

Pictured here is Gina Ventresca Carano. Born in Pratola Peligna, L'Aquila, Abruzzo, she was a musical prodigy, excelling at her scholastic studies at Germantown High School while pursuing vocal training at the prestigious Curtis Institute. She traveled extensively throughout Italy, especially her native Abruzzo, collecting ancient folk songs. She was one of the foremost authorities on Italian folk music, costumes, and traditions. She met with and sang for King Umberto II, the last king of Italy, at the Warwick Hotel on his visit to Philadelphia in 1963 and, later, at his villa in Cascais, Portugal, on the outskirts of Lisbon, by special request. She married noted Philadelphia lawyer Frank Carano, from the Italian settlement of Overbrook in West Philadelphia. She performed at the 1939 New York's World Fair and in 1976 at Memorial Hall during the city's bicentennial celebrations. (Courtesy of Norman Giorno-Calapristi.)

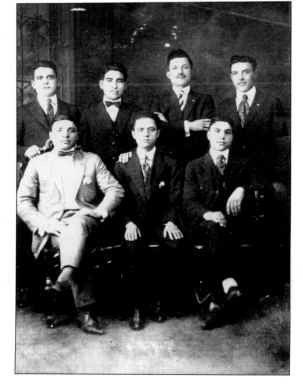

Group pictures, such as this c. 1915 photograph, were a way for Italian immigrants to reinforce old friendships while making a new life in the United States. Immigrants normally posed with *pisans*—people who were from the same town. Noelle Torchio, Luigi Giorno, Luardo Braccoli, Giuseppe Gardi, Frank Tosti, and Rosario Dima were part of a group of men from Luzzi, Cosenza, Calabria, who immigrated to Germantown in the early 1900s. (Courtesy of Norman Giorno-Calapristi.)

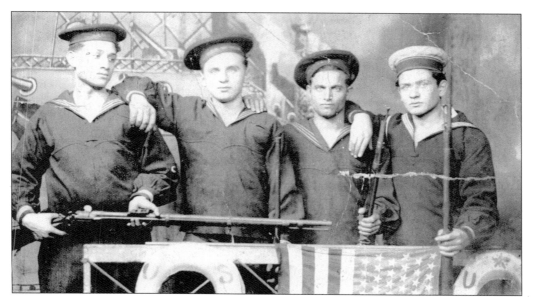

Local residents pose for this *c.* 1910 group picture. Pictured here, from left to right, are Nicola Cupo, Antonio Famularo, unidentified, and Ernesto M. Strollo. They were all from Palomonte, Salerno, Campania. (Courtesy of Joanne Strollo.)

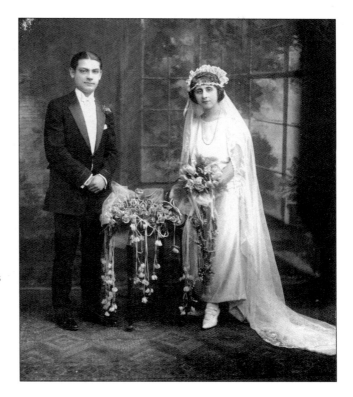

Pictured here is the wedding of James De Luca and Helen D'Avanzo in 1921. In the 1920s, immigrants and their children began to intermarry with Italians from other regions more than in previous years. James De Luca was born of parents from Altomonte, Cosenza, Calabria, and Helen immigrated from Palomonte, Salerno, Campania. (Courtesy of Norman Giorno-Calapristi.)

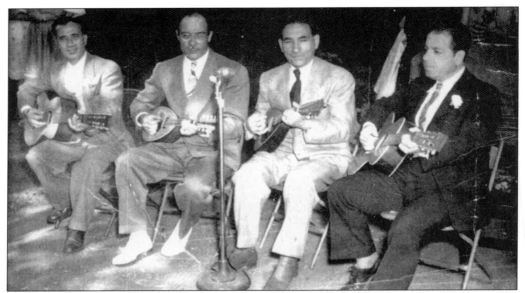

The Giorno Mandolin and Guitar Quartet is shown here in 1948. The musicians, from left to right, are Bill Berardi, Joe Grosso, Luigi Giorno, and Tony Colangelo. Quartets mainly consisting of two guitars and mandolins were usually employed for midnight serenades beneath the window of potential brides. If the woman liked the man, she would open her window after two or three songs and her family would invite him into the home. If she did not, the window remained closed. (Courtesy of Norman Giorno-Calapristi.)

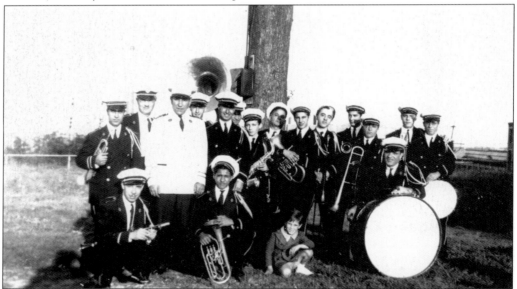

The Germantown Community Band was led by maestro Luigi Giorno. Symphonic bands were a staple at parish *festas*, providing the music for the procession of statues through neighborhood streets. The faithful would pin money to the statues, for charity's sake and/or for a divine favor. After the procession, the band played symphonic and classical music for the parishioners either in the street, in the playground, or in another performance area. (Courtesy of Norman Giorno-Calapristi.)

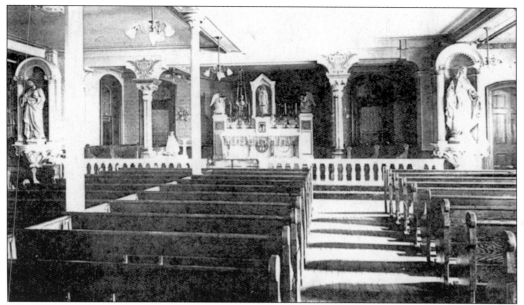

The Holy Rosary Chapel for Italians was established as the basement chapel for Italian parishioners in 1894. Fr. Secundus Lavizeri, C. M. (Congregation of the Mission), was the parish's first pastor. He is buried in the basement crypt of the building, which is now the perpetual Shrine of Our Lady of the Miraculous Medal, at 500 East Chelten Avenue. (Courtesy of Ducournau Archives, St. Vincent's Seminary.)

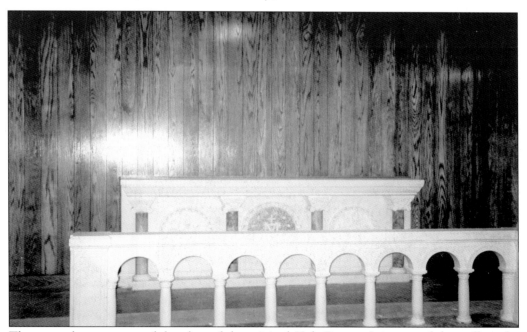

These are the remnants of the altar of the original Holy Rosary. It is part of the wall in the basement of the Shrine of Our Lady of the Miraculous Medal, 500 East Chelten Avenue. (Courtesy of Norman Giorno-Calapristi.)

✝

REV. SECUNDUS LAVIZERI, C.M.
NATUS DIE 23ª JULII 1825º
OBIIT DIE 5ª JUNII 1915º
VOCATIONIS 64º
REQUIESCAT.

Fr. Secundus Lavizeri, C.M., was the first pastor of Holy Rosary parish, founded in 1894. He is buried in the basement crypt of the Shrine of Our Lady of the Miraculous Medal. He was born on July 23, 1825, and died on June 5, 1915. The church moved to Haines Street and Belfield Avenue in 1927. The longest-serving pastor was Fr. Dominic Nepote, and Fr. Stephen India, the pastor at the time of Holy Rosary's closing in 1977, is still fondly remembered by former parishioners. (Courtesy of Norman Giorno-Calapristi.)

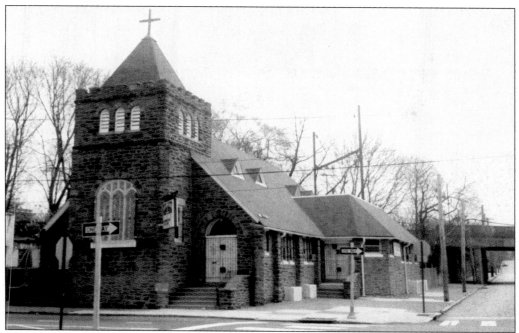

The stone building that was erected on the corner of Haines Street and Belfield Avenue in 1927 is pictured here. Holy Rosary was the Italian national parish for Italians of upper Germantown (St. Michael of the Saints was the parish for lower Germantown Italians) and Chestnut Hill. It was closed by the Archdiocese of Philadelphia in 1977. (Courtesy of Norman Giorno-Calapristi.)

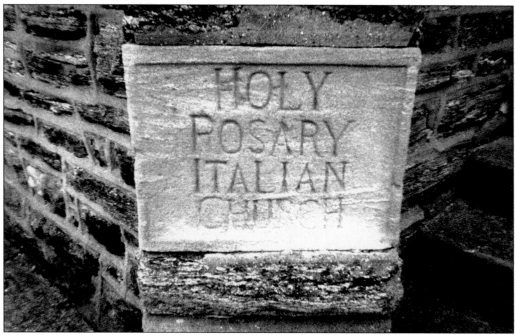

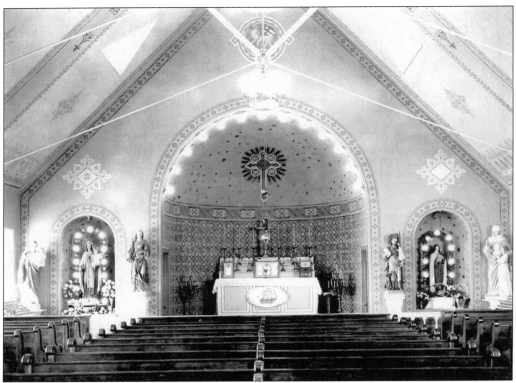

This is an interior view of Holy Rosary, Haines Street and Belfield Avenue, around the late 1920s and early 1930s. Due to concerns from women who wanted to walk through a middle aisle during their wedding, the pews were cut through to make a center aisle. (Courtesy of Joanne Strollo.)

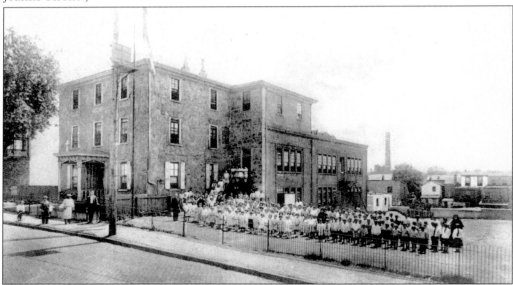

This exterior shot of the parish school of Holy Rosary, located at 334 East Haines Street, was taken in 1925. (Courtesy of Temple University Libraries, Urban Archives.)

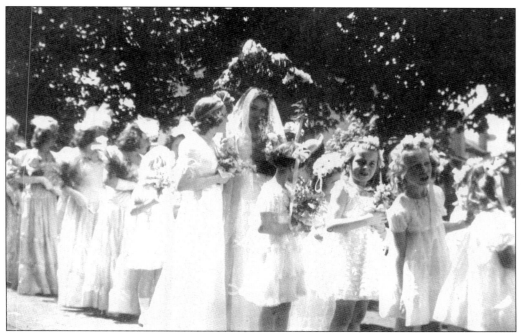

This Holy Rosary May procession took place in the late 1940s to early 1950s. (Courtesy of Chenza Iannuzzi Cerrato.)

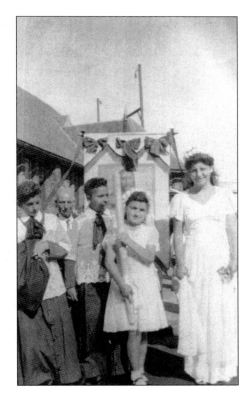

Seen here are processions during one of the *festas* of Holy Rosary. (Courtesy of Chenza Iannuzzi Cerrato.)

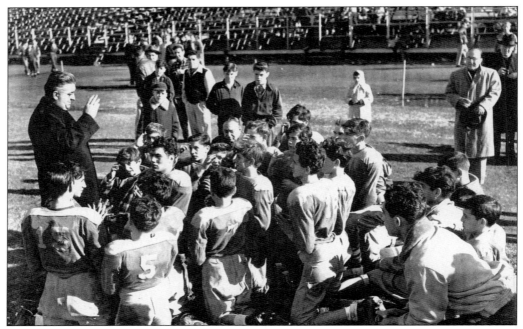

Fr. Culbert gives a blessing to the Holy Rosary football team before the start of the game around the mid-1950s. (Courtesy of Chenza Iannuzzi Cerrato.)

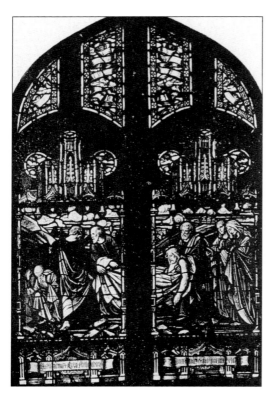

This intricate stained-glass window was created by noted stained glass maker Nicola D'Ascenzo. This is a window in St. Mark's Church in the Frankford section of the city. (Courtesy of Celeste A. Morello.)

Seen here is the Giuseppe Giusti Lodge No. 683 of the OSIA at 439 East Haines Street. It was incorporated in 1929 and eventually merged with the Luzzi lodge to form the Germantown lodge. The lodge was renamed the Strollo Lodge, in honor of Ernesto M. Strollo, who was fervently dedicated to the OSIA. The building was demolished in the 1960s. (Courtesy of Joanne Strollo.)

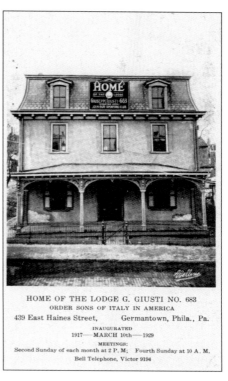

HOME OF THE LODGE G. GIUSTI NO. 683
ORDER SONS OF ITALY IN AMERICA
439 East Haines Street,   Germantown, Phila., Pa.
INAUGURATED
1917——MARCH 10th——1929
MEETINGS:
Second Sunday of each month at 2 P. M;   Fourth Sunday at 10 A. M.
Bell Telephone, Victor 9194

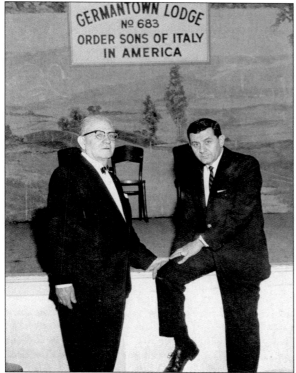

Ernesto M. Strollo and his son Michael were the first father and son treasurers of the Grand Lodge of Pennsylvania. (Courtesy of Joanne Strollo.)

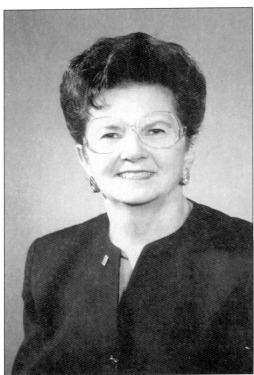

Joanne Strollo remains the only female national president in the 100-plus-year history of the OSIA. She served as national president from 1993 to 1995. (Courtesy of Joanne Strollo.)

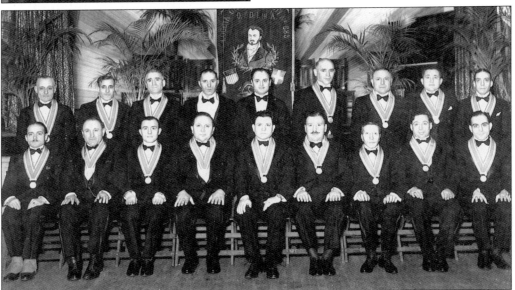

Officers of the Germantown Lodge No. 683 of OSIA are pictured here in 1937. Shown from left to right are the following: (first row) Reno Volpiani, Frank Medicino, Louis Cissone, Jimmy Ventresca, Ernest Strollo, Whitey Lorenzo, Jerry Fortunato, Vito Leonardo, and Phillip Coppola; (second row) Albert Corvino, Archie Sirianni, Joseph Bisigano, Sam Faino, Vincent Zimbaldi, Anthony Paolucci, Carmine Di Maria, Mariano Patelmo, and Frank Audino. (Courtesy of Joanne Strollo.)

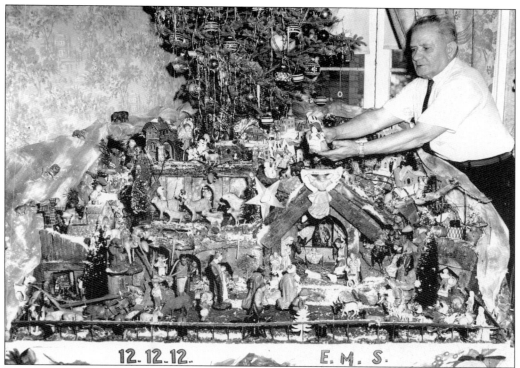

Ernesto M. Strollo puts the finishing touches on his elaborate *presepio*, the Italian Nativity scene. For every Christmas from 1912 to 1967, he set up the precepio every year and added to it throughout the years. His daughter Joanne inherited the elaborate scene. (Courtesy of Joanne Strollo.)

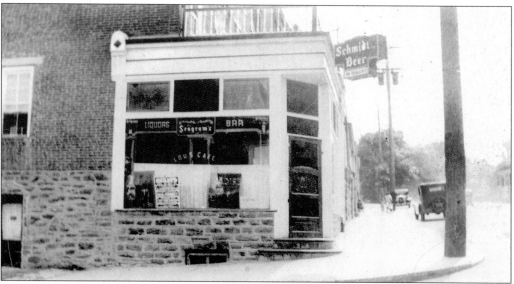

Lou's Café was run by Luigi Giorno at the corner of High and Magnolia Streets. It was a popular neighborhood hangout until its closure in 1948. This photograph is from 1940. (Courtesy of Mary Giorno De Maria.)

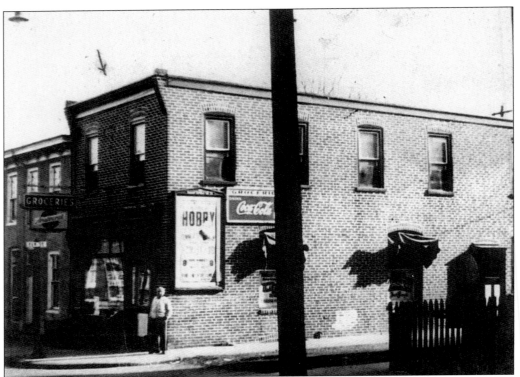

Di Luca's grocery store is pictured here. In later years, it was converted into a Laundromat, the advertisement for which appeared in the Holy Rosary parish bulletin. (Courtesy of Theresa Criniti De Cristofano.)

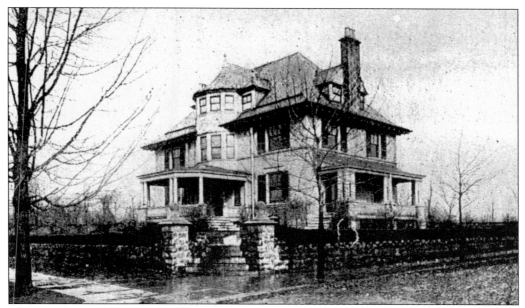

This is an 1899 photograph of 5801 Chew Avenue, which became the Errichetti Funeral Home. Proprietor Victor J. Errichetti's father, Antonio, started the funeral home on Salmon Street in Port Richmond. Victor eventually moved to Germantown, where he ran his very successful, and much beloved, funeral parlor until his death on April 7, 1972. (Courtesy of Norman Giorno-Calapristi.)

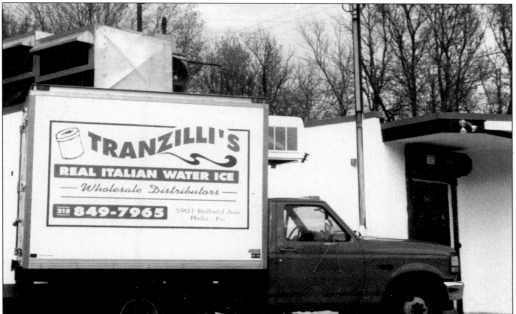

The Tranzilli family was late in coming to Germantown, having settled in the neighborhood in the late 1950s or early 1960s. They still run a very successful water ice stand at Haines Street and Belfield Avenue, directly across the street from the former Holy Rosary Church, to this day. (Courtesy of Norman Giorno-Calapristi.)

Sylvio Tino and Ralph Cauterucci were very successful pharmacists in Germantown. Their successful completion of the rigorous requirements of pharmacy school is testament to the determination of Italian immigrants to succeed in their new country.

Italian businesses continued to successfully operate in Germantown into the 1960s, as these advertisements from a 1965 Holy Rosary parish bulletin attest to.

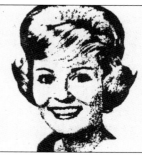

J. D. Pessano

Law, Collections.
Real Estate and
Conveyancing,

No. 23 W. Chelten Ave., Gtn.

City Office: 907 WALNUT ST., Phila.

Telephone No 845   18 Years Experience.

**WE WILL COLLECT YOUR
RENTS for 3 PER CENT.**
We Make a Return Monthly.

J. D. Pessano ran a real estate agency near Germantown and Chelten Avenues in 1894.

The Girard Beef Company

"LA MACELLERIA DEGLI ITALIANI DI
GERMANTOWN

Il nostro Motto:

"DARVI IL VALORE DEL VOSTRO DENARO CON
CARNI FRESCHE OGNI GIORNO"

GIRARD - BEEF COMPANY

5821 GERMANTOWN AVENUE   PHILADELPHIA, PA.

The Girard Beef Company proclaims to be the butcher shop for Germantown Italians in this advertisement from 1927.

Charles Deatore advertised his tailor shop in the short-lived *North Philadelphia Globe* newspaper on May 7, 1942. Centrella's Live Poultry made its services known in the January 30, 1941, edition of the newspaper.

The Scubbi Funeral Home was a funeral home in Germantown that serviced primarily Italians. Another prominent funeral home was that of Leandro N. Angelone, who is still in business today. (Courtesy of Norman Giorno-Calapristi.)

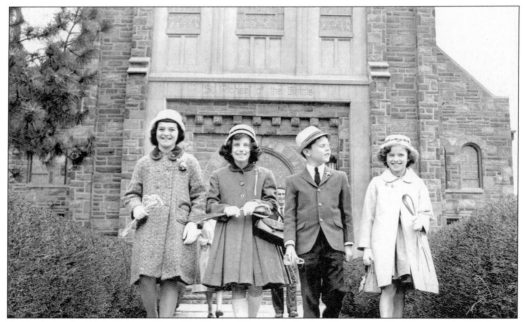

From left to right, Donna Zanolli, Kathy Bianconi, Rudy Vigilante, and Rosemary Vigilante are dressed in their Sunday best for Palm Sunday services in 1963 at St. Michael of the Saints Church, 4811 Germantown Avenue. The settlement of Italians on lower Germantown Avenue, nicknamed the "Brickyard," were mainly from Reggio (the southernmost province of the region of Calabria), various towns in the provinces of Salerno and Avellino in Campania, and the extreme northeastern region of Friuli-Venezia Giulia. (Courtesy of Temple University Libraries, Urban Archives.)

From left to right, Louisa D'Avanzo, Clare D'Avanzo, Alexis D'Avanzo, Vincent D'Avanzo, Helen De Luca, and Vincentine De Luca stand in front of the ornate grotto of St. Michael's Church in lower Germantown. (Courtesy of Norman Giorno-Calapristi.)

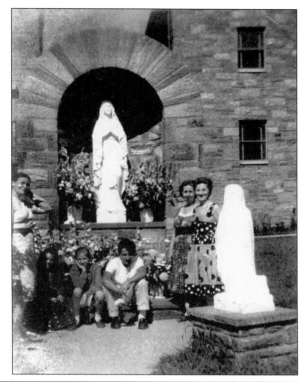

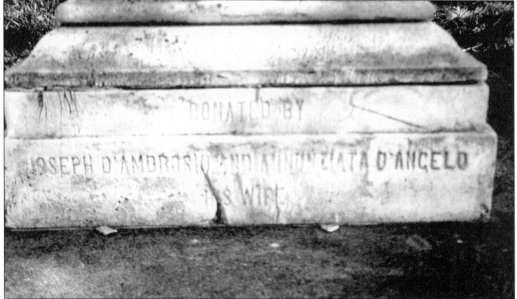

Italians gave ornate gifts to the church in thanks for any divine favors they may have asked for. Sometimes they would pay for a stained-glass window for the church, and other times they would pay for ornate statues to be placed on the grounds of the church. This is the base of a statue located on the former grounds of St. Michael's, which is now gone, donated by Joseph D'Ambrosio and Annunziata D'Angelo. (Courtesy of Norman Giorno-Calapristi.)

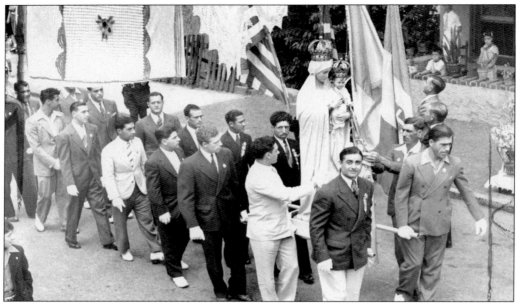

Parishioners of St. Lucy's in Manayunk carry the statue of Our Lady of Mount Carmel for the Feast of the Sacred Heart in 1940. The highlight of an Italian national parish's calendar, the festa can last from one to three days. Celebrations include carnival rides and games of chance and are run by the clubs and sodalities of the parish. (Courtesy of Temple University Libraries, Urban Archives.)

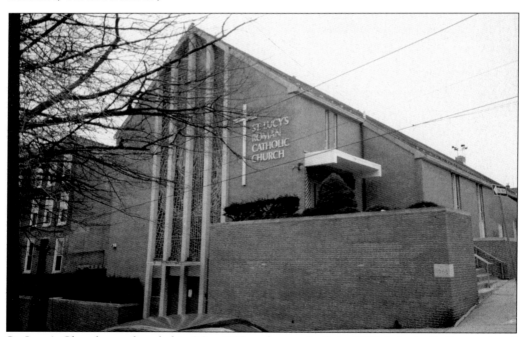

St. Lucy's Church was founded in May 1927 and was rebuilt in 1968. It is the Italian national parish of Manayunk and neighboring East Falls. St. Lucy is the patron saint of the city of Naples, but immigrants from several regions settled in both neighborhoods. (Author's collection.)

The statue of St. Lucy (Santa Lucia) is pictured at the side altar of St. Lucy's Church. St. Lucy was a popular saint in the city of Naples and surrounding communities and the patroness of those afflicted with eye ailments. She is featured holding her eyes, which were ripped out by the Romans for preaching Christianity, in a plate. Side altars, or statue rooms, are unique to Italian Catholic churches, as many of the saints in those rooms are Italian. (Author's collection.)

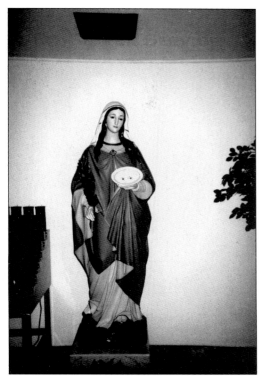

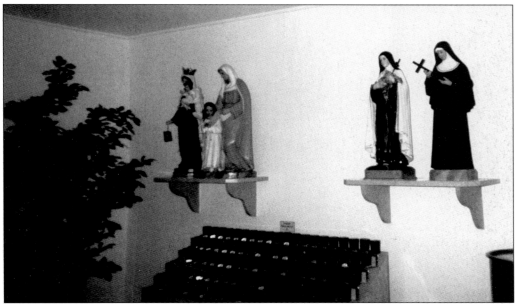

Pictured here is another shot of the side altar of St. Lucy's. From left to right are the statues of Our Lady of Mount Carmel, St. Anne and the child Mary (mother of Jesus), St. Therese of the Little Flower, and St. Rita of Cascia. These statues could either represent where many immigrants came from in Italy or were saints of popular devotion that many parishioners were devoted to. (Author's collection.)

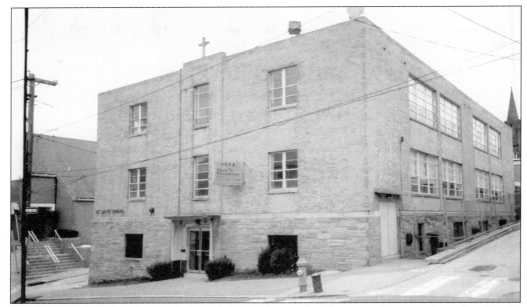

The former school building of St. Lucy's, located immediately across the street from the church, is seen here. The sale sign is indicative of the decreasing enrollment in Catholic schools in the inner city. The school was closed by the Archdiocese of Philadelphia in 2005, merging with the parish schools of Holy Family, St. Mary of the Assumption, and St. Josaphat. The merged school is called Holy Child. (Author's collection.)

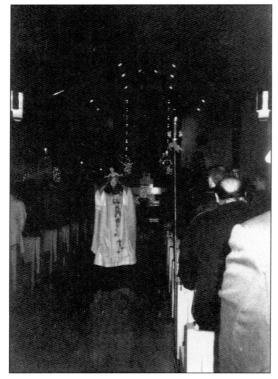

Pictured here is Christmas Eve mass at St. Lucy's in December 2006. Fr. Francis Sabatini, pastor, continues the traditional Italian Christmas Eve mass by parading the baby Jesus around St. Lucy's church to the accompaniment of the Italian Christmas hymn "Tu Scendi dale Stelle." (Author's collection.)

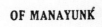
These advertisements are from the *Manayunk Review* of 1939 and 1940.

Meri's Cafe
4632 Umbria St.

Famous Italian Submarines]
10c - 15c - 25c

Spaghetti Anytime

Tru-Blu & Schmidt's Beer
Liquor   Wine

MERI AND SAM AT THE TAPS

These advertisements for Italians businesses appeared in the *Manayunk Review* in 1941 and 1942.

Your Part in the Drive for Victory

All Material for DEFENSE

Paper - Iron - Metal - Rags
Old Tires and Tubes

E. J. MENARDI
Shop · 4649 Umbria Street
Bell Phone: Rox. 2106-W

Where Old Friends Meet, Drink & Eat

Louie's Famous Italian
Submarine Sandwiches
Wimpy's Dream Hamburger Eaters 10c-15c
Curb Service
We Specialize in Steak
Sandwiches 10c-15c
Hot Roast Beef 5c-10c
Hamburgers 5c-10c
Fish Cakes 5c-10c
Texas Weiners 10c

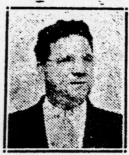

Cooper's and True Blu Beer on Tap. Wines, Whiskey and Gin and Mixed Drinks. Biggest Bar in Town.

We Serve Spaghetti and Chow Mein

LOUIE'S CAFE

Established Over 20 Years

Man. 1844   **4632 Umbria St**

These are from the May 24, 1939, edition of the *Manayunk Review*.

DeGOVANN'S CAFE

—

FEATURING
THE 3 NOTES
FRI. & SAT. NITES
SANDWICHES
SEAFOOD PLATTERS SOUPS
SPAGHETTI OUR SPECIALTY
TRY OUR FOOD

—

4630 Umbria St., Myk.
Phone MAN. 9184

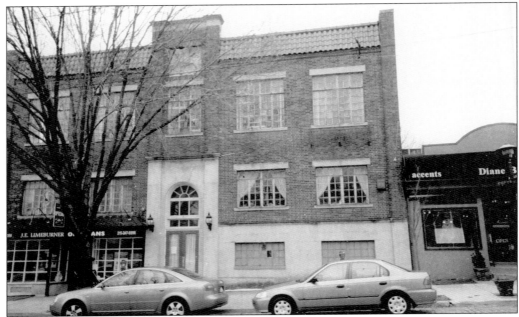

The exterior of the Venetian Social Club is shown here. Founded in October 1924, its main purpose was to reinforce the bonds between those of Venetian heritage. It later included many social activities, including the singing of Venetian and Friulani folk songs. The club enjoys continued success to this day. (Author's collection.)

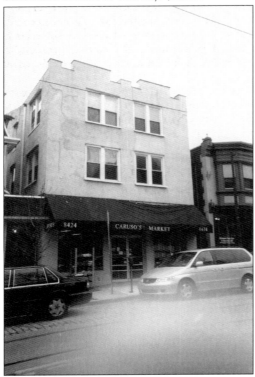

This is a well-known mecca for the Italians of Mount Airy and Chestnut Hill. It features a variety of imported and domestic products. (Author's collection.)

Three

The Italians
of Northeast
Philadelphia

The histories of the Italian enclaves of Frankford and Tacony share common names. The first pastor of Our Lady of Consolation (OLC) was Fr. Alfredo Procopio, who was an assistant to Fr. Cosmas Bruni, pastor of Mater Dolorosa in Frankford. According to the parish history of OLC, in September 1917, Archbishop Prendergast instructed Procopio to establish an Italian church in Tacony, to which he obliged. The original church was located at Wellington and Edmund Streets. Its present building, located at 7056 Tulip Street, was the site of the Giovanelli home, which Mabel Giovanelli gave up with a heavy heart. During the Depression, the church almost closed, but Fr. James V. Rosica, a native of Mater Dolorosa, was able to pull it back from the brink of closure and make it a viable parish once again. Today OLC continues to thrive, and Tacony itself retains a small but active Little Italy.

The same cannot be said of the enclave of Frankford. It lives on in spirit today, but no begging needs to go on to get former residents to reminisce about their neighborhood. Mater Dolorosa struggles to survive in an ever-changing neighborhood with various social programs to assist the community. Its parish school suffered the fate of many inner-city Catholic schools and closed in June 2004. Former students now attend Holy Innocents Area Catholic School in nearby Juniata Park.

Port Richmond's Italian enclave continues to thrive to this day. It still supports famous businesses such as Taconelli's Pizzeria, Italian-named funeral homes such as Cassizzi and Gallo, barbershops, and so on. Their Italian national parish, Mother of Divine Grace, continues to thrive, and the neighborhood has an active Sons of Italy lodge.

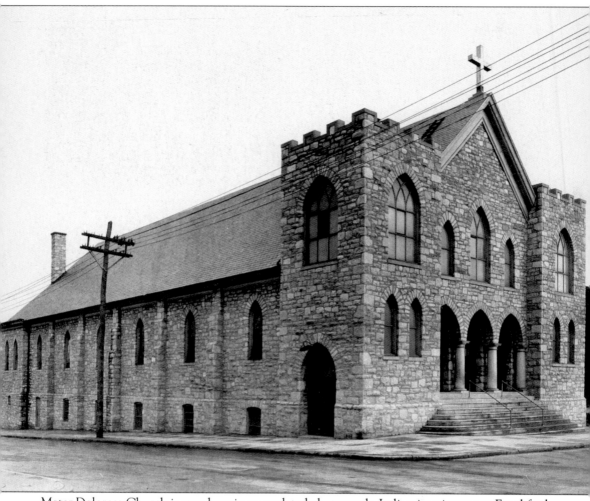

Mater Dolorosa Church is seen here in an undated photograph. Italian immigrants to Frankford, as with Italians all over the city, felt unwelcomed at American Catholic churches, run overwhelmingly by Irish clergy, for their brand of Catholicism. They petitioned the Archdiocese of Philadelphia to establish an Italian national parish in Frankford, which was granted. A national parish was designed to serve the unique needs of a particular immigrant group. Anyone of that ethnic origin could join the church, no matter where they lived. The first Italian church of Frankford was founded in February 1908 and christened St. Peter. Masses were held in a storefront house, starting in March 1908, by the first pastor, Father Santoro. The church changed names twice in 1911. In April, parishioners selected the name of St. Rocco (its full name was St. Rocco's Chapel for Frankford Italians), and in December, they permanently settled upon Mater Dolorosa (Latin for "sorrowful mother," the mother being the Virgin Mary, mother of Jesus). The church was built in 1914. It continues to serve the Frankford community today through its various social services. (Courtesy of Mater Dolorosa Parish.)

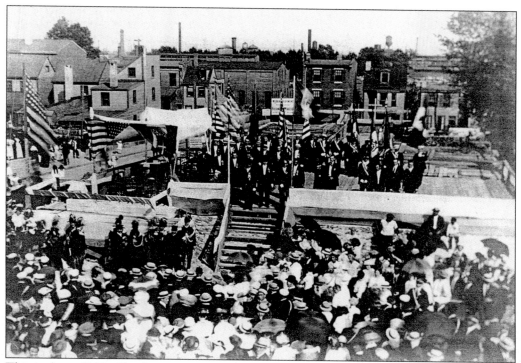

This is the *c.* 1908 official ceremony for the founding of Mater Dolorosa Church. (Courtesy of Mater Dolorosa Parish.)

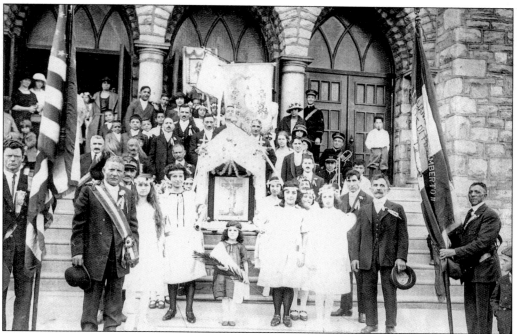

Mater Dolorosa parishioners celebrate the Feast of Santa Liberata in 1924. (Courtesy of Joe Mc Laughlin.)

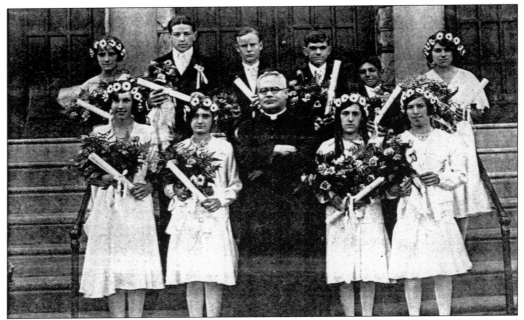

The first graduating class of Mater Dolorosa School is shown in 1930. The school educated thousands of neighborhood children in Frankford from its founding in 1926 until its closing in June 2004. Former students now attend Holy Innocents Area Catholic School in the Juniata Park section of the city. (Courtesy of Mater Dolorosa Parish.)

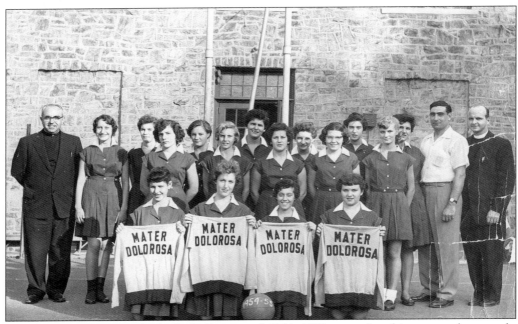

The Mater Dolorosa girls' basketball team of 1954–1955 poses for this group photograph. (Courtesy of Mater Dolorosa Parish; photograph by Robert Kennedy.)

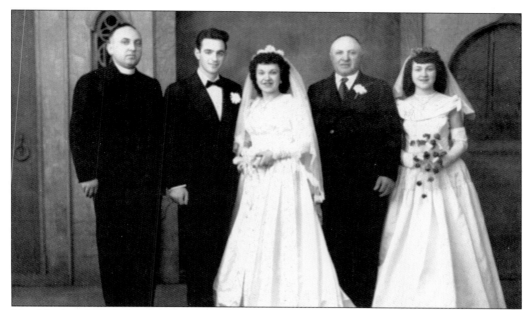

Neighborhood Catholic churches were the center of social activities and major life events, such as baptisms, weddings, and funerals for immigrants and their children. This is the December 31, 1949, wedding of Frankford residents and Mater Dolorosa parishioners William Monteleone and Louise Veneziale. Also pictured are, from left to right, Fr. Antimo Veneziale, Gaetano Veneziale, and Rose Veneziale. (Courtesy of Mater Dolorosa Parish.)

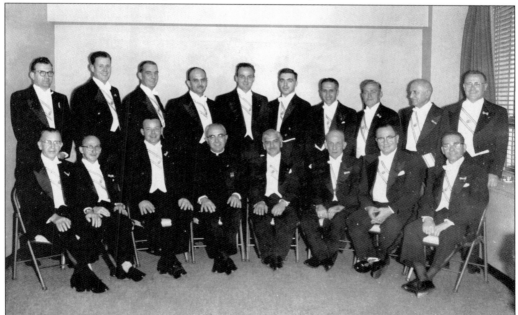

Pastor Fr. Albert Palumbo is in this c. 1960 picture with the local Knights of Columbus. The Knights of Columbus is a Catholic fraternal beneficial organization headquartered in New Haven, Connecticut, open to Catholic men, regardless of ethnicity. (Courtesy of Mater Dolorosa Parish.)

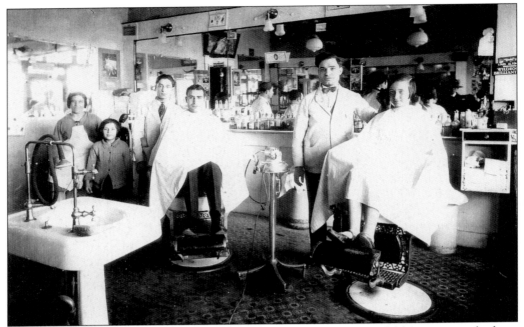

Many Italian immigrant men throughout Philadelphia set up successful businesses as barbers. Pictured here is the barbershop of Luigi Altomari, located at 4611 Torresdale Avenue. Also pictured are his wife, Francesca, and daughter Antoinette. (Courtesy of Lou Altomari.)

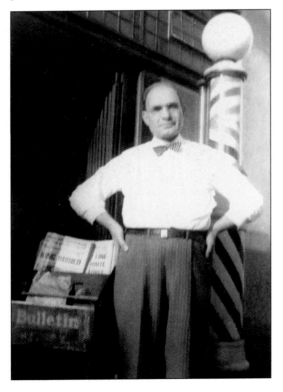

Luigi Altomari was a legendary barber in Frankford. He served the neighborhood for many years, cutting an untold number of heads, until his retirement in 1968. (Courtesy of Lou Altomari.)

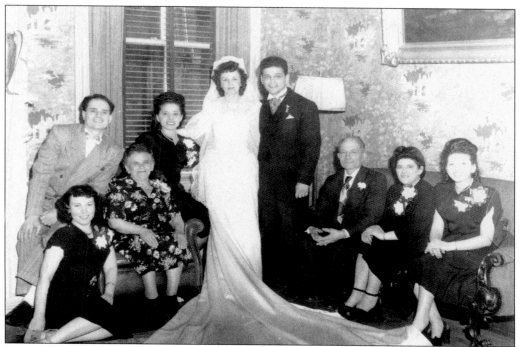

Pictured here is a c. 1946 Dagastino family wedding. (Courtesy of Eileen Mc Shane Miller.)

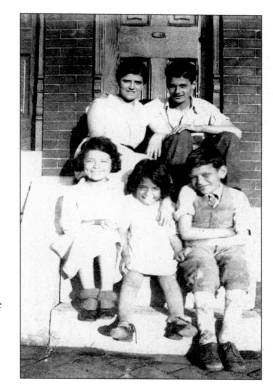

The Dagastino family poses for a group picture on its stoop at 4309 Leiper Street around 1931. The children were products of the beginning of Italians marrying outside of their ethnicity, as their father was Irish. (Courtesy of Eileen Mc Shane Miller.)

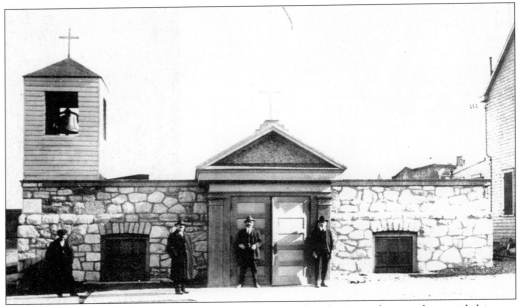

This is the first building of Our Lady of Consolation Church. According to the parish history, Fr. Alfredo Procopio borrowed $10,000 in 1917 to build the church. (Courtesy of the Historical Society of Tacony.)

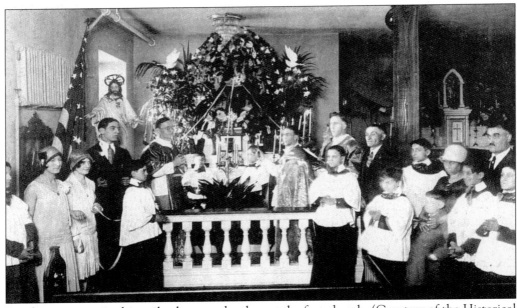

Parishioners pose in this early photograph taken at the first church. (Courtesy of the Historical Society of Tacony.)

Fr. Alfredo Procopio was the assistant to Fr. Cosmas Bruni, pastor of Mater Dolorosa Church in Frankford. In 1917, Archbishop Edmund Prendergast instructed Procopio to head a new Italian national parish in neighboring Tacony for the increasing number of Italians settling there to be named Our Lady of Consolation. According to parish history, the early settlers of Tacony were from the province of Cosenza in the region of Calabria. (Courtesy of the Historical Society of Tacony.)

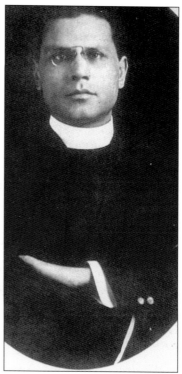

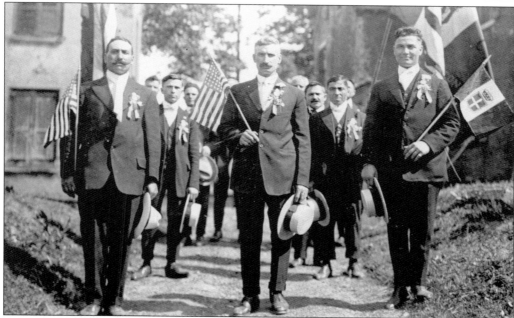

Parishioners of OLC march in the procession for the Feast of Santa Liberata. Note the Italian flag on the right-hand side is that of the Kingdom of Italy. St. Liberata is the patron saint for the town of Rogliano, Cosenza, Calabria, which is where many of the OLC parishioners could have ancestry (or that of surrounding towns). (Courtesy of the Historical Society of Tacony.)

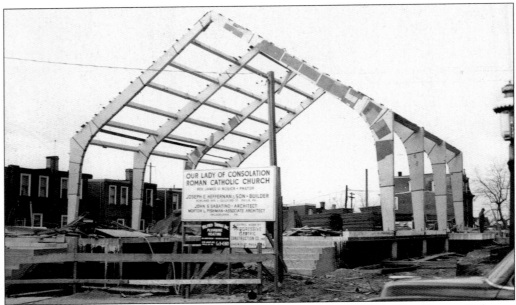

The newly erected framework of the new OLC church is shown here. The Giovanelli home, located on the 7000 block of Tulip Street, was selected as the site of the new church. Fr. James V. Rosica told Mabel Giovanelli that her home would need to be demolished to make room for a new church. After initial reluctance to give up her dream home, she finally consented. (Courtesy of the Historical Society of Tacony; photograph by Larry Trombetta.)

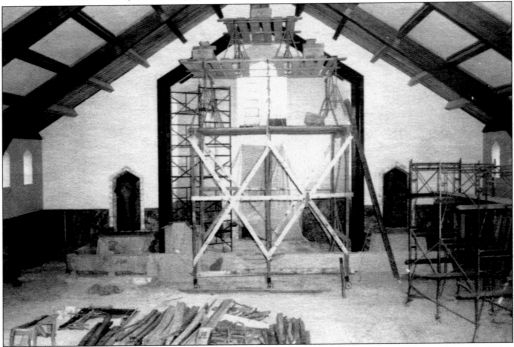

The still unfinished chapel of the new church at 7056 Tulip Street is seen on November 11, 1956. (Courtesy of the Historical Society of Tacony; photograph by Larry Trombetta.)

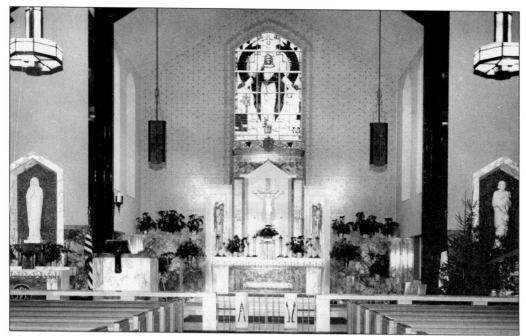

The finished altar of OLC is pictured here. The present-day church was built by Philadelphia architects John Sabatino and Morton Fishman. (Courtesy of the Historical Society of Tacony; photograph by Larry Trombetta.)

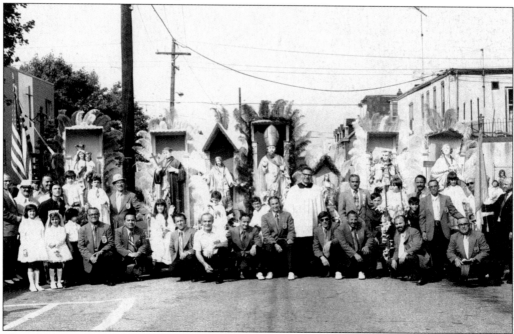

This photograph was taken during the annual Feast of the Seven Saints—St. Liberata, St. John, St. Lucy, Sacred Heart, Our Lady of Mount Carmel, St. Anthony, and St. Donato. (Courtesy of the Historical Society of Tacony; photograph by Larry Trombetta.)

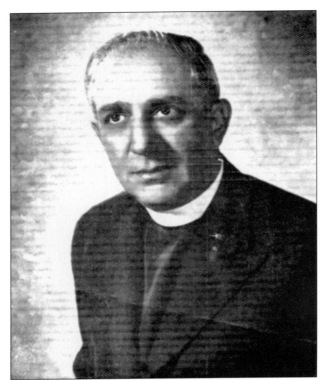

Fr. James V. Rosica was appointed pastor of OLC by Cardinal Dennis Dougherty only one year after being ordained. He grew up in Frankford and attended Mater Dolorosa. He pulled OLC from the brink of closure during the Great Depression and became the longest-serving pastor (1933–1971). (Courtesy of the Historical Society of Tacony.)

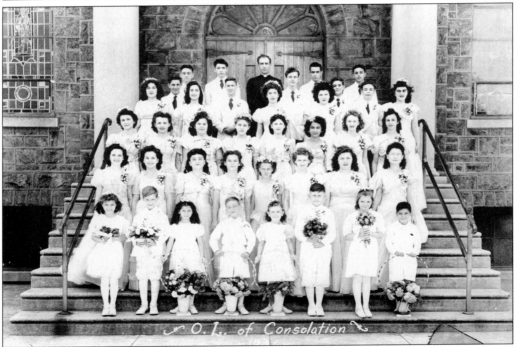

The graduating class of 1946 poses for this photograph at the parish school. (Courtesy of the Historical Society of Tacony.)

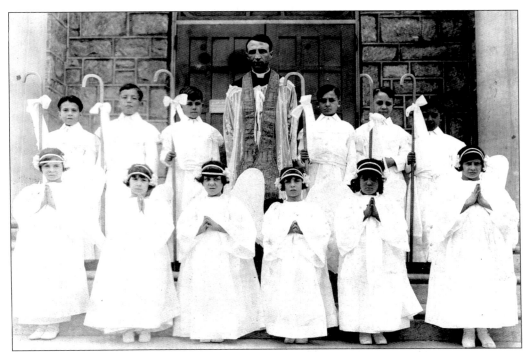

Fr. Agnello Angelini, second pastor of the church, poses on a 1927 feast day. (Courtesy of the Historical Society of Tacony.)

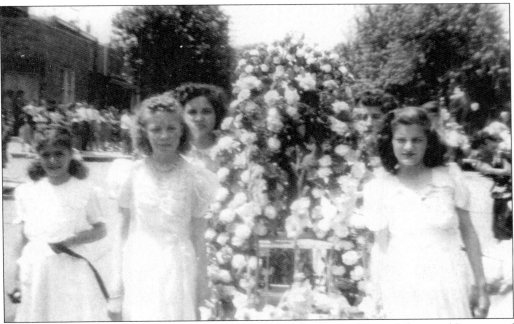

Schoolchildren carry a statue during the procession of the Feast of Santa Liberata. (Courtesy of the Historical Society of Tacony.)

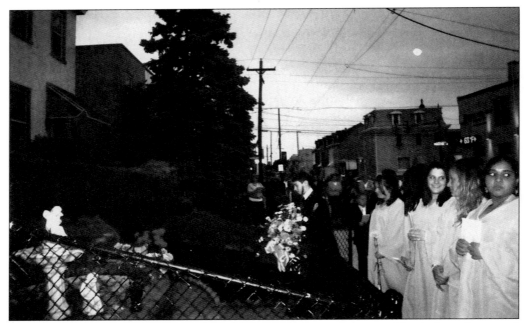

OLC continues to thrive in a time of parish closures and consolidations. This is from the annual May procession, taken on May 12, 2006. (Courtesy of Louis Iatarola.)

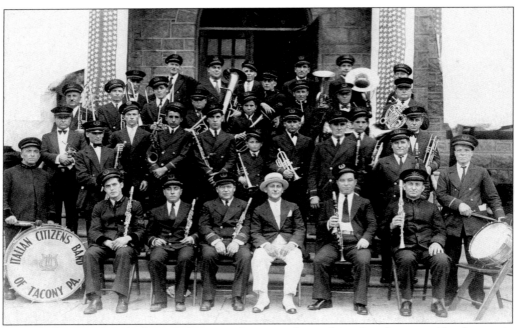

Every Italian enclave had an Italian symphonic and marching band to provide the music for the festas. Germantown had the Germantown Community Band led by Luigi Giorno, Twenty-second Street had Mr. Tamburrino, and South Philadelphia had Giuseppe Bardascino and La Banda Lozzi, among numerous others. The Italian Citizens Band of Tacony poses in this undated photograph. (Courtesy of the Historical Society of Tacony.)

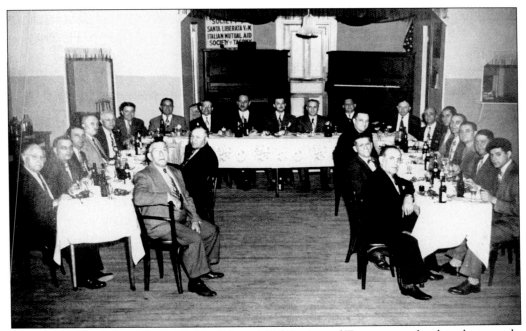

The men of the Santa Liberata Italian Mutual Aid Society of Tacony pose for this photograph. Mutual aid societies were created to provide members with life insurance and decent funerals. They were initially set up to help immigrants from a particular town but later grew to include Italians from every region. (Courtesy of the Historical Society of Tacony.)

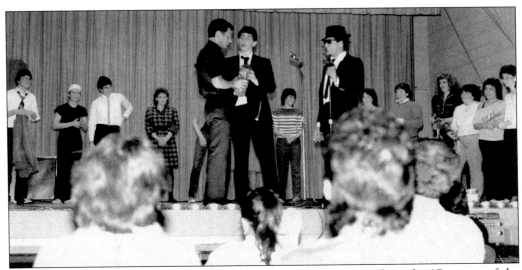

Pictured here is an OLC school play from the 1980s, starring Louis Iatarola. (Courtesy of the Historical Society of Tacony.)

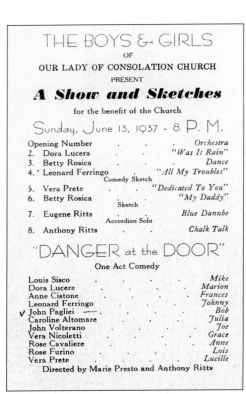

THE BOYS & GIRLS

OF

OUR LADY OF CONSOLATION CHURCH

PRESENT

A Show and Sketches

for the benefit of the Church

Sunday, June 13, 1937 - 8 P. M.

Opening Number	.	.	Orchestra
2. Dora Lucera	.	.	"Was It Rain"
3. Betty Rosica	.	.	Dance
4. Leonard Ferringo	.	.	"All My Troubles"
	Comedy Sketch		
5. Vera Prete	.	.	"Dedicated To You"
6. Betty Rosica	.	.	"My Daddy"
	Sketch		
7. Eugene Ritts	.	.	Blue Danube
	Accordion Solo		
8. Anthony Ritts	.	.	Chalk Talk

"DANGER at the DOOR"

One Act Comedy

Louis Sisco	.	.	.	.	Mike
Dora Lucera	.	.	.	.	Marion
Anne Cistone	.	.	.	.	Frances
Leonard Ferringo	.	.	.	.	Johnny
John Pagliei ———	.	.	.	.	Bob
Caroline Altomare	.	.	.	.	Julia
John Volterano	.	.	.	.	Joe
Vera Nicoletti	.	.	.	.	Grace
Rose Cavaliere	.	.	.	.	Anne
Rose Furino	.	.	.	.	Lois
Vera Prete	.	.	.	.	Lucille

Directed by Marie Presto and Anthony Ritts

This program is from a 1937 play held at the church. (Courtesy of the Historical Society of Tacony.)

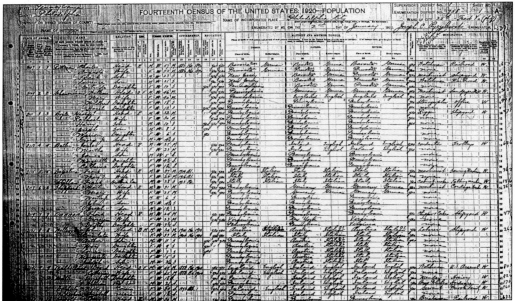

This page from the 1920 census shows that the streets surrounding Port Richmond's Little Italy were ethnically mixed. Some Italian immigrants even felt comfortable enough to marry non-Italians as early as the second decade of the 20th century, as the marriage between an Italian immigrant woman and an Austrian immigrant man, of 3121 Almond Street, demonstrates. (Courtesy of the National Archives and Records Administration, Mid-Atlantic Region.)

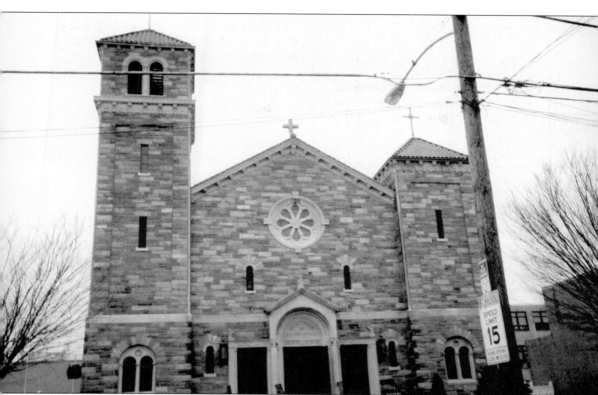

Pictured here is Mother of Divine Grace Church. In 1918, Fr. Charles Bruni established St. Rocco's Chapel for Italians, at Ontario and Amber Streets, to serve the spiritual needs of Italian immigrants in Port Richmond. By 1926, Fr. John Colantoni was appointed pastor of the newly formed Mother of Divine Grace Church. Colantoni commenced a survey to establish where the largest settlement of Italians was located in order to commence construction of a church building. It was decided that the largest settlement was located near Amber and Somerset Streets, so a church was built on nearby Thompson Street. Today the parish thrives, along with three other parishes in Port Richmond (the Polish national parish of St. Adalbert, Our Lady Help of Christians, and Nativity Blessed Virgin Mary). It hosts an annual Italian festival, held in late May, and a spaghetti dinner to benefit the parish, and a healthy number of students attend the parish school. (Author's collection.)

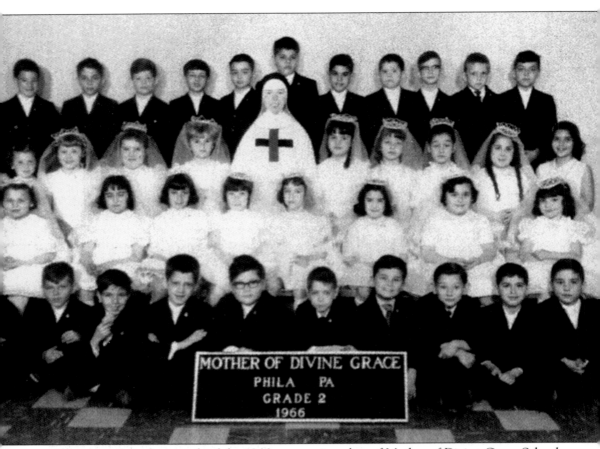

This is the class photograph of the 1966 communion class of Mother of Divine Grace School. (Courtesy of Juliana Di Pasquale Giordano.)

The Errichetti Funeral Home, begun by Antonio Errichetti, has its roots in Port Richmond. As the number of Italian immigrants increased in the city, and along with older people dying off and the high rate of infant mortality, there was an increasing need for Italian funeral parlors to know how to properly deal with grieving Italian families. Antonio's son, Victor, eventually moved the funeral home to Germantown. (Courtesy of Norman Giorno-Calapristi.)

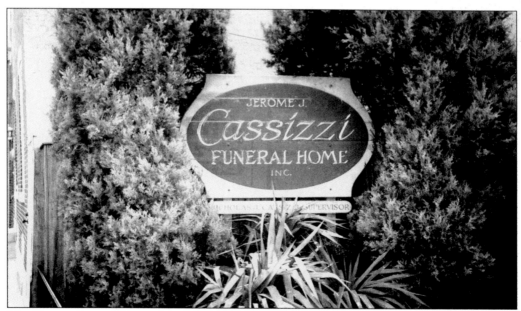

The Cassizzi Funeral Home, located on East Thompson Street, has been serving Port Richmond Italians, and the community as a whole, for many years. It is located directly across the street from Mother of Divine Grace Church, allowing people a glimpse of how establishments used to be within walking distance of each other in industrial Philadelphia. (Author's collection.)

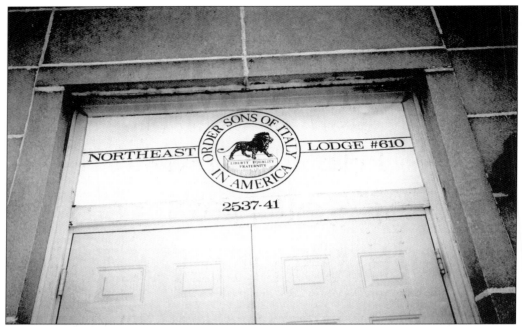

The Port Richmond Lodge No. 610 of OSIA enjoys a healthy and active membership. The OSIA was established in 1905 as a mutual aid society and has grown to become the largest and oldest organization for men and women of Italian heritage in the United States. (Author's collection.)

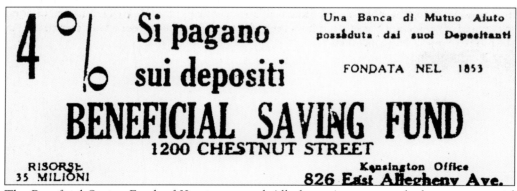

The Beneficial Saving Fund, of Kensington and Allegheny Avenues, reached out to potential Italian customers in Port Richmond (and throughout the city) via *La Libera Parola* in the July 21, 1928, edition of the newspaper.

Four

THE ITALIANS OF SOUTHWEST PHILADELPHIA AND WEST PHILADELPHIA

Not much information exists regarding the Italian enclaves of Southwest Philadelphia (Our Lady of Loreto Parish) and Overbrook.

It is known that Overbrook was a very active Italian neighborhood. It supported three Italian national parishes (St. Donato, Our Lady of the Angels, Our Lady of the Rosary) and the social clubs, funeral homes, and businesses that were staples of an Italian neighborhood.

Today, although many Overbrook Italians have since moved out of the neighborhood (primarily to Delaware County), there remains Italians around Sixty-fifth and Callowhill Streets as well as Italian-owned businesses and clubs, such as Caffé Sportivo Italiano, Morrone Water Ice, and Haverford Furniture (owned by Italian Americans), among other businesses.

The settlement that constituted the parish of Our Lady of Loreto is, unfortunately, not well documented. Despite vigorous attempts to obtain information regarding this settlement in Southwest Philadelphia, none could be found. The former residents of this neighborhood (around the area of Sixty-second Street and Grays Ferry Avenue) should document their community in the future to give it its proper due.

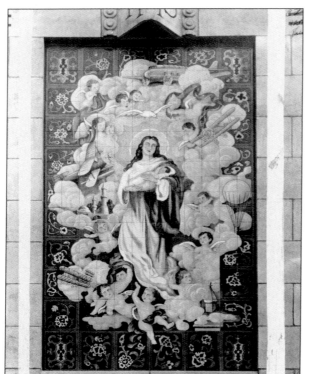

Located at Sixty-second Street and Grays Ferry Avenue in Southwest Philadelphia, the church of Our Lady of Loreto sported a beautiful tower, which was designed by Frank A. Petrillo. Loreto is a town in the region of Marche, in central Italy, and is home to the Holy House of Loreto, one of the most popular shrines in Italy. It is unknown where many of the immigrants who settled in Southwest Philadelphia emigrated from in Italy. The church was one of the last Italian national parishes to be established in the city, opening in 1932 and closed by the Archdiocese of Philadelphia in 2000. (Courtesy of Temple University Libraries, Urban Archives.)

This is a census page for a portion of a block of Callowhill Street, Overbrook. It shows a pattern established in the city and all over the country: immigrants tended to settle in clusters, living right next to one another, possibly in an effort to keep their ethnic identity and to feel comfortable living among other Italians, more specifically pisans—people from their own towns. (Courtesy of the National Archives and Records Administration, Mid-Atlantic Region.)

St. Donato's Church, located at Sixty-fifth and Callowhill Streets, is shown in 1922. The other two were Our Lady of the Rosary (closed by the Archdiocese of Philadelphia in 2005) and Our Lady of the Angels (closed in 2006). (Courtesy of Temple University Libraries, Urban Archives.)

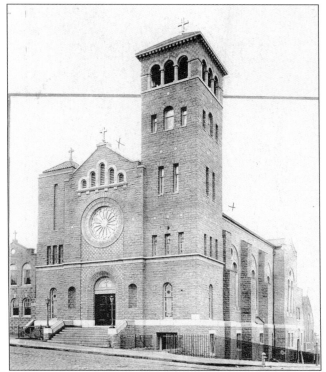

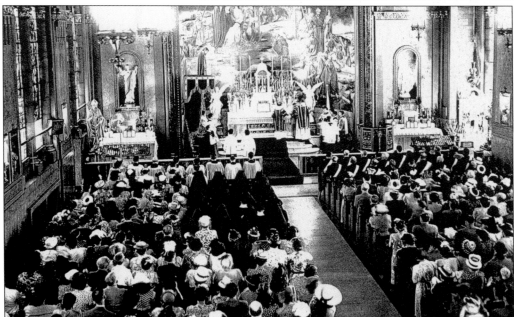

The interior of St. Donato's, a Gothic-style church, is seen here. The altar is decorated with a life-size painting of the Crucifixion. Prior to the establishment of St. Donato's, parishioners worshipped at Our Mother of Sorrows, located at Forty-eighth Street and Lancaster Avenue. (Courtesy of Temple University Libraries, Urban Archives.)

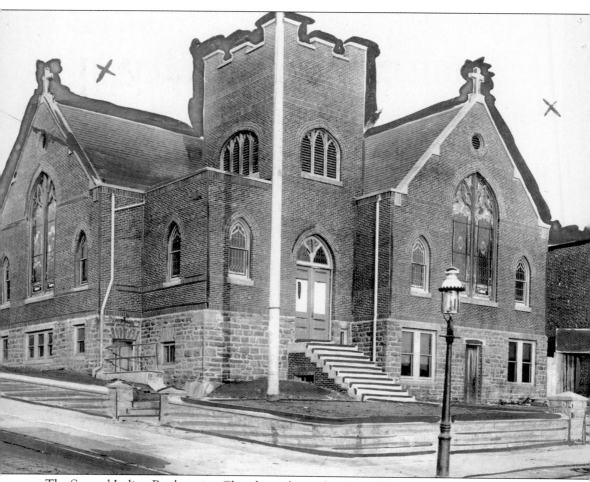

The Second Italian Presbyterian Church was located at Sixty-fifth and Callowhill Streets. After the success of the First Italian Presbyterian Church in South Philadelphia, the Presbytery of Philadelphia expanded its mission to the Italian Catholic area of West Philadelphia. Beginning as the Christian Italian Mission in November 1905, it was successful enough to have church trustees build a new church in a lot adjacent to St. Donato's in 1908. In 1910, it was renamed Second Italian Presbyterian Church of Philadelphia. The mission peaked with over 250 members but rapidly declined as the second and third generations quickly assimilated and moved from the neighborhood. The church name was changed to St. Andrew and St. Philip Presbyterian Church in 1948, as it remains today. (Courtesy of Temple University Libraries, Urban Archives.)

The language of music is Italian, and Italians have a knack for teaching, playing, and selling music. These advertisements are from the *Overbrook Times* and *Overbrook Mirror* newspapers from the 1940s.

GR 3-3072

Music For All Occasions

JOSEPH CROCCO
921 N. 64th St.

Concert   Swing
Band & Orchestra   Orchestra

DiSTEFANO'S MUSIC SHOP
RADIOS — RECORDS
CARDS — GIFTS — TOYS
ELEC. APPLIANCES REPAIRED
6505 Lansdowne Ave., TRI. 1883

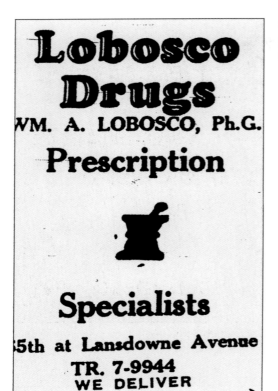

This advertisement for Lobosco Drugs at Sixty-fifth and Callowhill Streets appeared in the *Overbrook Times* on March 27, 1947.

Here is an advertisement from the *Overbrook Mirror* on September 12, 1940.

This advertisement appeared in *La Libera Parola* on February 4, 1928.

Here is an advertisement from the *Overbrook Times* on May 30, 1946.

Vincent Amoroso

6309 Lansdowne Ave.

TAILOR & FURRIER

GRE. 1290

This is an advertisement from the *Overbrook Mirror* June 20, 1940, issue.

This advertisement is from the June 13, 1940, issue of the *Overbrook Mirror*.

Five

THE ITALIANS OF NORTH PHILADELPHIA

Again, not much information could be found regarding the settlements of Twenty-second Street, and Sixth Street and Erie Avenue. These are two neighborhoods that deserve to be written about to fill in the blanks regarding immigration patterns, the early settlers, and so on.

From documents such as marriage licenses and citizenship papers, it can be said that immigrants began settling in the area of Twenty-second and Clearfield Streets as early as the 1880s. It was a small enclave but very active. The neighborhood supported at least two Italian funeral homes in its heyday (Di Giacomo and Nicastro) and scores of Italian restaurants, clubs, and varied businesses (one Italian-owned business, Dave's Meat Market, remains on North Twenty-second Street to this day and is quite successful).

The majority of Italian Americans moved out of the area by the late 1960s, many moving to the Roxborough section of the city. Many former parishioners of St. Mary of the Eternal are now active members of Immaculate Heart of Mary Church in Roxborough. I.H.M. is even home to a plaque commemorating men from St. Mary's who died in World War II.

Information about the Sixth Street and Erie Avenue enclave is almost nonexistent. For shame, because Sciolla's bar and club called this section of the city (named Tioga) home. Sciolla's was just as famous as Palumbo's, although not as oft-mentioned as the latter.

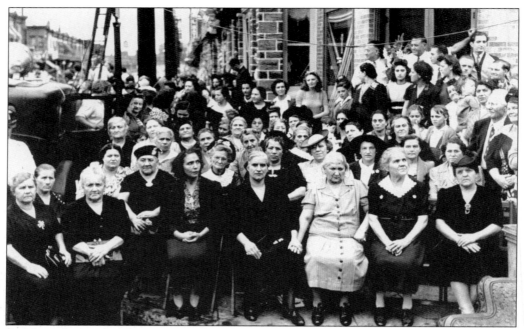

St. Mary's Ladies Sodality is pictured on the corner of Twenty-first Street and Indiana Avenue. Among the women are Mary Salvia (front row, last seat on the right) and Jennie Marmero (second row, third from the right). Sodalities were separated by sex and helped the church in various charitable and social endeavors. (Courtesy of Denise Di Antonio.)

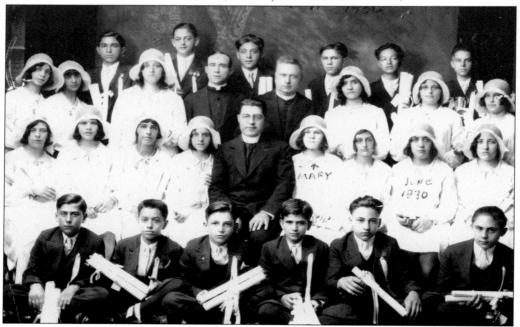

St. Mary of the Eternal's eighth-grade class of 1930 is pictured here. The priest is Father Palumbo, the first pastor of the church. Also in the class are Louis Di Giacomo (standing, second from left) and Mary Marmero (to the right of Palumbo). (Courtesy of Denise Di Antonio.)

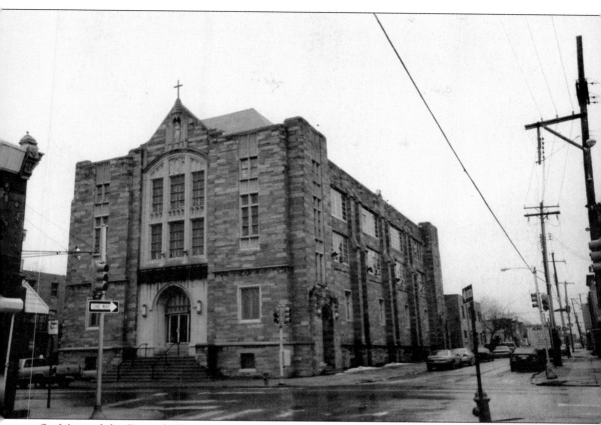

St. Mary of the Eternal Church was located at Twenty-second and Clearfield Streets in North Philadelphia. The design of this church is unique because the school was part of the same building as the church (located on the right-hand side on Clearfield Street). The cornerstone was laid in 1929, shortly before the start of the Great Depression. The church was named after a sanctuary of the same name, Santuario di Maria Santissima dell'Eterno, in Montecorvino Rovella, Salerno, Campania, where many of the immigrants to "Twenty-second Street" (as it is popularly referred to) were from. There was also a healthy settlement of Italians who were from the provinces of L'Aquila and Chieti, in the region of Abruzzo, as well as immigrants from Molise (which became its own region in 1963. Before then, the province was identified as Abruzzo and Molise, and many immigrants were labeled as Abbruzzese). At one time, the church boasted thousands of member families, but by the early 1970s, with urban flight in full gear, the church struggled. The Archdiocese of Philadelphia closed the parish in 1976. (Author's collection.)

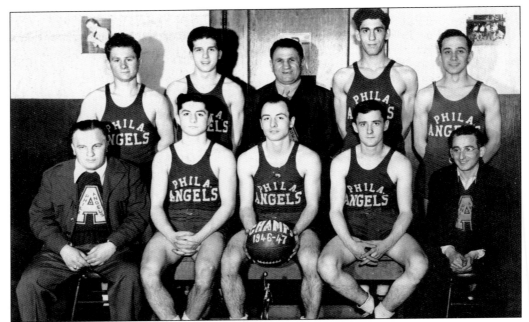

The Philadelphia Angels, a neighborhood basketball team, are pictured here. From left to right are (seated) Fred "Cici" Marmero, Larry Chiodetti, Tom Cheeseman, Alfred "Goggi" Buonviso, and unidentified; (standing) John Laurenzi, Lou De Cesare, Arturo "Cat" Giargiari, Frank Leonardo, and "Mertz" Vasso. (Courtesy of Denise Di Antonio.)

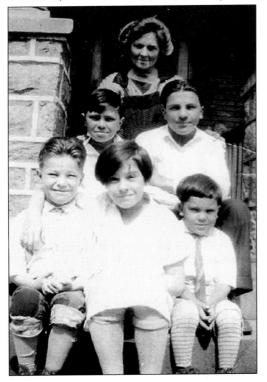

A trademark of industrial Philadelphia row house life was sitting on the stoop and chatting with neighbors or just taking the opportunity to relax. The Marmero family took advantage of its row house stoop at 3026 North Woodstock Street for a casual family photograph. From top, left to right, are Jennie, John, Fred, Ben, Mary, and Joe Marmero. (Courtesy of Denise Di Antonio.)

The May procession is the annual honoring of the Virgin Mary. In Italian parishes, a girl from the eighth grade is selected to "crown" a statue of Mary, and the communion classes of that year parade behind her. Anna Marmero, Mary Peets, and Mary Marmero are among those photographed for St. Mary's May procession around 1923. (Courtesy of Denise Di Antonio.)

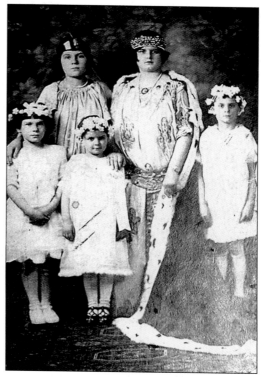

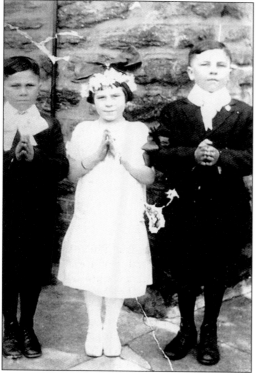

Communion is an important occasion for Italian Catholics, and Catholics in general, as it signifies the right to receive the communion wafer distributed during mass. It welcomes younger Catholics into a more participatory role in mass. Pictured here are, from left to right, John Mermero, Mary Mermero, and Alfred Marmero on their communion day around 1924–1925. (Courtesy of Denise Di Antonio.)

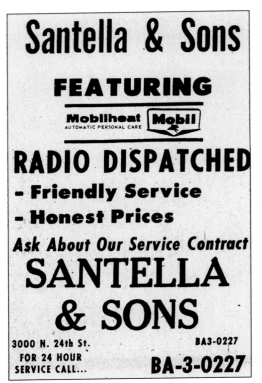

Santella & Sons

FEATURING

Mobilheat · Mobil
AUTOMATIC PERSONAL CARE

RADIO DISPATCHED

- Friendly Service

- Honest Prices

Ask About Our Service Contract

SANTELLA & SONS

3000 N. 24th St.   BA3-0227
FOR 24 HOUR
SERVICE CALL...   **BA-3-0227**

With constant images of suburbia put across to the public as being more ideal than living in the city, and urban flight to the suburbs beginning to increase in the 1950s, Italian businesses continued to successfully operate in North Philadelphia into the 1960s. Santella and Sons oil company ran a large advertisement in the February 14, 1963, edition of the *Nicetonian* weekly newspaper.

Cell Phone, Tioga 8563 R.

Ser. De Matthaeis

Ph. G.

PHARMACIST

3600 No. 22nd St., Phila., Pa.

The Italian community of Philadelphia was vibrant enough to warrant a few Italian-language newspapers that served the community for years. Italian businesses were successful enough to continually advertise in these publications for weeks on end, and some businesses advertised in them for years. This advertisement for pharmacist De Matthaeis at 3600 North Twenty-second Street ran in *La Libera Parola* on January 8, 1927.

This is a present-day picture of the building that once was Our Lady of Pompeii Church. Located at Sixth Street and Erie Avenue, it was founded in 1914 as the Italian national parish of the Tioga section of the city. It was closed by the Archdiocese of Philadelphia in June 1993. The building now houses Solomon Temple Baptist Church. (Author's collection.)

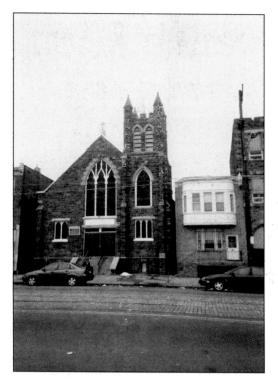

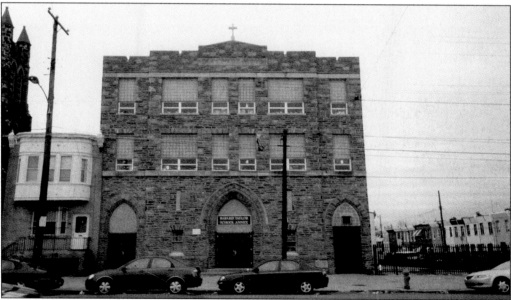

This building was once Our Lady of Pompeii parish school. Located just two buildings from the church, it was an example of how schools, churches, and businesses were within walking distance of immigrants' homes, making it virtually unnecessary to go outside of one's neighborhood for the essentials, the idea behind a "Little Italy." The building is now the annex for the Richard Taylor public school. (Author's collection.)

Pictured here is the citizenship petition of Luigi Di Giacomo, who became a U.S. citizen on March 30, 1903. He was one of the earliest settlers to the area of Twenty-second and Clearfield Streets and the grandfather of Louis Di Giacomo, the original proprietor of the Di Giacomo Funeral Home. His citizenship petition shows that, prior to mass immigration, little more information than the name of the petitioner, his present address, what country he came from, and the name and address of one person who served as a character witness was required. With the explosion of immigrants arriving to Philadelphia and the United States in general in the first decade of the 20th century, this would drastically change. Immigrants were to supply more detailed information regarding themselves and their families, as well as needing two character witnesses. (Courtesy of the National Archives and Records Administration, Mid-Atlantic Region.)

The citizenship petition for Angelo Coia, born in Cerasuolo, Naples, Italy, shows how the federal government required much more information from immigrants during and after mass immigration. By the second decade of the 20th century, immigrants were required to show their ship arrival papers (stating where they sailed from, on what boat, and when they arrived to the United States) and state what town they were from in their native country, in addition to providing detailed information regarding the birth dates and birthplaces of their wives and children, and the names and addresses of two witnesses attesting to the character of the petitioner. All of this information was obtained in an effort to keep track of what countries immigrants were coming from and would be used to justify severely limiting immigration from southern and eastern Europe with the Immigration Control Act of 1924. Today such detailed information on these citizenship forms is a genealogist's treasure trove. (Courtesy of the National Archives and Records Administration, Mid-Atlantic Region.)

SCIOLLA'S RHYTHM BA

521 WEST PIKE STREET
— FEATURING —
"THE 3 TONES"—NIGHTLY

COCKTAIL HOUR SATURDAY, 2 to 6 P. M.
HARD-SHELL CRABS   SHRIMP
Most Delicious Italian Spaghetti In Town!
TONY SCIOLLA, Mgr.   RAD. 9556   Ample Parking Spa

Sciolla's, located at Fifth and Pike Streets, was on par with Palumbo's in South Philadelphia when it came to delicious food, entertainment, and visits from a seemingly endless stream of celebrities. Philadelphia-born pop singer Bobby Rydell made his nightclub debut at Sciolla's in May 1961. This advertisement is from the May 7, 1942, edition of the short-lived *North Philadelphia Globe* newspaper.

Spero's Café offered turkey platters for an unbeatable 35¢, in addition to a full line of beer and liquors. This is from the *North Philadelphia Globe* of January 30, 1941.

Local businesses advertised in weekly neighborhood newspapers as a means of keeping their business visible. The bigger the advertisement, the more successful the business presumably was. This advertisement for Borghesi Coal was published in the January 30, 1941, edition of the *North Philadelphia Globe* newspaper.

MICCUCI'S PIZZERIA
CORNER 6th & PIKE STS.

YOU TASTED THE REST — NOW TRY THE BEST.

YOU CALL
WE DELIVER

BA 8-9928

HOURS
DAILY FRO
4 P.M.-1 A.M

Italian businesses continued to thrive in Tioga into the mid-1960s. This advertisement for Miccuci's Pizzeria is from the June 4, 1964, edition of the *Nicetonian*.

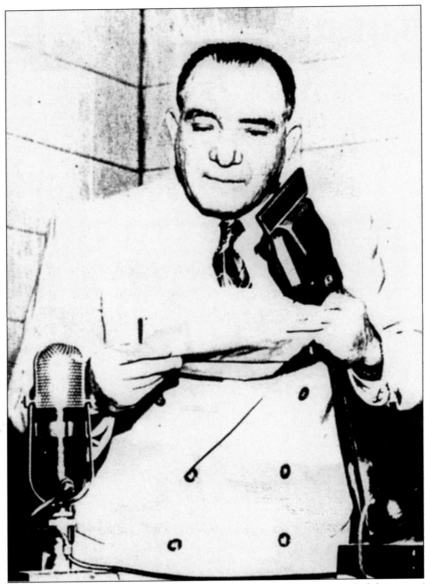

Frank Trombetta was born in Santa Caterina del Ionio, Catanzaro, Calabria in 1890. He immigrated to South Philadelphia, where he died in 1973. From 1932 until 1961, he hosted an Italian-language radio program on WHAT-AM in Philadelphia. In 1961, he went to WTEL-AM, where he was the Italian broadcast director and announcer until his death. He was musically inclined since childhood, mastering the mandolin, and organized several orchestras during his career. He received the title of Cavaliere dell,Ordine della Croce di Savoia (Cavalier of the Order of the Cross of the House of Savoia, the royal house of Italy) from King Umberto II, the last king of Italy, a rare honor in the United States. He was also honored by the Italian Republic with the Cavaliere dell,Ordine della Stella di Solidarieta della Republica Italiana (Cavalier of the Order of the Star of Italian Solidarity). Both titles are awarded to people who foster goodwill between Italy and the United States and who distinguish themselves by their talents in the field of Italian culture and service to the Italian community. (Courtesy of Norman Giorno-Calapristi.)

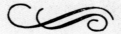
The Errichetti Funeral Home distinguished itself with a unique appointment by the Italian government. It was chosen to be the funeral home for Pennsylvania and New York State in the event that an Italian official died while in the United States. It is a rare honor awarded to a funeral home. (Courtesy of Norman Giorno-Calapristi.)

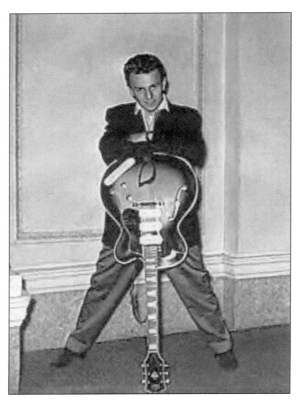

Charlie Gracie is seen at the legendary London Palladium in the 1950s. He was the first successful musician to emerge from South Philadelphia. He was one of the earliest pioneers of rockabilly, an early form of rock and roll that emerged in the United States in the 1950s. Rockabilly's origins lay heavily in blues, swing, and country (or "hillbilly") music, which was popular in the American South. Gracie was a legend all over Europe, especially in England, and was preceded only by Billy Haley. He eventually became good friends with, and mentor to, an up-and-coming band by the name of the Beatles. He recorded with them in the famed Abbey Road Studios and has remained friends with them ever since. Although a legend in Europe, his contribution to music stateside has gone largely unnoticed and unappreciated. (Courtesy of www.charliegracie.com.)

Although he was born in South Philadelphia, it is fitting that the final picture in this book should be that of Thomas Michael Foglietta. From 1997 to 2001, he received a great honor when he was named by Pres. Bill Clinton as the U.S. ambassador to Italy. He graduated from South Catholic High School in 1945 and earned a bachelor of arts degree from St. Joseph's College in 1949 and his doctor of laws degree from Temple University Law School in 1952. He was elected as the youngest person to Philadelphia City Council in 1955, where he would serve for 20 years (1955–1975), was regional director for the Department of Labor in 1976, and served in Congress first as an independent then as a Democrat, staying in Congress for seven terms (1981–1997). He resigned in 1997 to take on the role of ambassador to Italy. He died in 2004 and is buried in Holy Cross Cemetery, in Yeadon, Delaware County.

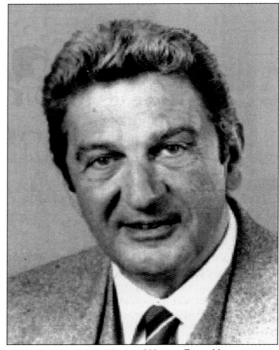

BIBLIOGRAPHY

Calapristi, Norman Giorno. "A Brief History of Holy Rosary Church." *Germantown Crier.* Fall 2004.

De Wolf, Rose. "Strong Italian Flavor Here." *Philadelphia Daily News*, August, 1, 1984.

Dubin, Murray. *South Philadelphia Mummers, Memories, and the Melrose Diner.* Philadelphia: Temple University Press, 1996.

Form, William. "Italian Protestants: Religion, Ethnicity, and Assimilation." *Journal for the Scientific Study of Religion* 39, no. 3 (September 2000): 307–320.

Gennaro, Lorraine. "Christian Churches." *South Philadelphia Review.* March 17, 2005.

Hammonds, Kenneth A. *Historical Directory of Presbyterian Churches and Presbyteries of Greater Philadelphia: Related to the Presbyterian Church (U.S.A.) and Its Antecedents, 1690–1990.* Philadelphia: Presbyterian Historical Society, 1993.

Juliani, Richard N. *Building Little Italy, Philadelphia's Italians Before Mass Migration.* University Park, PA: Pennsylvania State University Press, 1998.

"Little Italy in Penn's City." Historical Society of Pennsylvania, Campbell Collection, Volume 64, page 106.

Obituary of Salvatore Massaro, *Philadelphia Evening Bulletin*, March 28, 1933.

Our Lady of Consolation Church, Philadelphia, Pennsylvania. South Hackensack, NJ: Custombook Inc., 1967.

Philadelphia Record, "Happenings of a Day in the City's Churches," August 10, 1914

Russoniello, Grace. *Italian-American Traditions: Family and Community.* Historical Society of Pennsylvania.

Saverino, Joan L. "Italians of Northwest Philadelphia: Remembering a Community's Past." *Germantown Crier.* Fall 2000.

———. "Memories in Artifact and Stone: Italians Build a Neighborhood." *Germantown Crier.* Fall 2003.

Webster, Daniel. "Philadelphia Composer Makes a Mark, Even after His Death." *Philadelphia Inquirer*, May 10, 1997, sec. B.

www.brynmawr.edu/cities/archx/05-600/proj/p2/jcecb/FirstItalian.html

www.consolationtacony.org/pages/history.shtml

www.cst-phl.com/060126/parish.html

www.history-of-rock.com/daily_events_1961.htm

www.motherdivinegrace.net/history.htm

www.newadvent.org/cathen/09762a.htm

www.osia.org/public/about/who_we_are.asp

www.saintritashrine.org/ritalife.htm

www.stnicksphila.com/history.htm

www2.hsp.org/collections/manuscripts/2100.htm

ACROSS AMERICA, PEOPLE ARE DISCOVERING SOMETHING WONDERFUL. *THEIR HERITAGE.*

Arcadia Publishing is the leading local history publisher in the United States. With more than 3,000 titles in print and hundreds of new titles released every year, Arcadia has extensive specialized experience chronicling the history of communities and celebrating America's hidden stories, bringing to life the people, places, and events from the past. To discover the history of other communities across the nation, please visit:

www.arcadiapublishing.com

Customized search tools allow you to find regional history books about the town where you grew up, the cities where your friends and family live, the town where your parents met, or even that retirement spot you've been dreaming about.

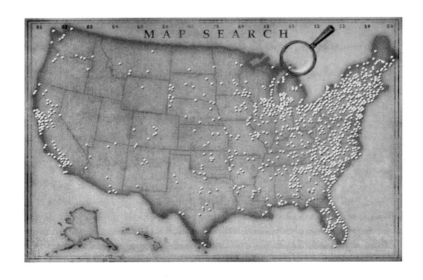